CAD IN CLOTHING AND TEXTILES

A Collection of
Expert Views

ALSO FROM BLACKWELL SCIENCE

Metric Pattern Cutting
Third Edition
Winifred Aldrich
0 632 03612 5

Metric Pattern Cutting for Children's Wear
Second Edition
Winifred Aldrich
0 632 03057 7

Metric Pattern Cutting for Menswear
Including Computer-aided Design
Second Edition
Winifred Aldrich
0 632 02635 9

Pattern Grading for Children's Clothes
The Technology of Sizing
Gerry Cooklin
0 632 02612 X

Pattern Grading for Men's Clothes
The Technology of Sizing
Gerry Cooklin
0 632 03305 3

Pattern Grading for Women's Clothes
The Technology of Sizing
Gerry Cooklin
0 632 02295 7

Introduction to Clothing Manufacture
Gerry Cooklin
0 632 02661 8

The Technology of Clothing Manufacture
Second Edition
Harold Carr and Barbara Latham
0 632 03748 2

Fashion Design and Product Development
Harold Carr and John Pomeroy
0 632 02893 9

Materials Management in Clothing Production
David J Tyler
0 632 02896 3

Knitted Clothing Technology
Terry Brackenbury
0 632 02807 6

CAD IN CLOTHING AND TEXTILES

A Collection of Expert Views

Second Edition

EDITOR

Winifred Aldrich

Blackwell
Science

© Winifred Aldrich 1992, 1994

Blackwell Science Ltd
Editorial Offices:
Osney Mead, Oxford OX2 0EL
25 John Street, London WC1N 2BL
23 Ainslie Place, Edinburgh EH3 6AJ
350 Main Street, Malden
    MA 02148 5018, USA
54 University Street, Carlton
    Victoria 3053, Australia
10, rue Casimir Delavigne
    75006 Paris, France

Other Editorial Offices:

Blackwell Wissenschafts-Verlag GmbH
Kurfürstendamm 57
10707 Berlin, Germany

Blackwell Science KK
MG Kodenmacho Building
7–10 Kodenmacho Nihombashi
Chuo-ku, Tokyo 104, Japan

First published 1992
Second edition 1994
Reprinted 1999

Set by Best-Set Typesetter Ltd,
Hong Kong
Printed and bound in Great Britain by
MPG Books Ltd, Bodmin, Cornwall

DISTRIBUTORS

Marston Book Services Ltd
PO Box 269
Abingdon
Oxon OX14 4YN
(Orders: Tel: 01235 465500
          Fax: 01235 465555)

USA
Blackwell Science, Inc.
Commerce Place
350 Main Street
Malden, MA 02148 5018
(Orders: Tel: 800 759 6102
               781 388 8250
          Fax: 781 388 8255)

Canada
Login Brothers Book Company
324 Saulteaux Crescent
Winnipeg, Manitoba R3J 3T2
(Orders: Tel: 204 837-2987
          Fax: 204 837-3116)

Australia
Blackwell Science Pty Ltd
54 University Street
Carlton, Victoria 3053
(Orders: Tel: 03 9347 0300
          Fax: 03 9347 5001)

A catalogue record for this title
is available from the British Library

ISBN 0–632–03893–4

Library of Congress
Cataloguing-in-Publication Data
is available

CAD in clothing and textiles:
a collection of expert views / editor,
    Winifred Aldrich. – 2nd ed.
        p.   cm.
    Includes index.
    ISBN 0–632–03893–4
    1. Costume design – Data
processing.
    2. Textile industry – Data
processing.
    3. Computer-aided design.
    I. Aldrich, Winifred.
TT507.C28   1994
677'.0285 – dc20   94-19280
                                              CIP

For further information on
Blackwell Science, visit our website:
www.blackwell-science.com

Contents

Contributors

WINIFRED ALDRICH, Pinewoods, Paterson Drive, Woodhouse Eaves, Leics LE12 8RL

CAROLINE ASHBY, CAD for CAD, Caroline Ashby Designs, 128 Shakespeare Road, London W3 6SW

DOUGLAS COOPER, PO Box 1907, Capetown 8000, South Africa

ROZ DAVIES, 2 Rawden Street, Camden Town, London NW1 0SU

JANE DEVANE, 27 Riversley Road, Elmsbridge, Gloucester GL2 0QS

STEPHEN GRAY, 18 Cowper Road, Harpenden, Herts AL5 5NG

KAREN MACHIN, Royal College of Art, Kensington Gore, London SW7 2EU

CHARLES SHENAFIELD, Tietex Corporation, 3010 North Blackstock Road, PO Box 6218, Spatanburg, SC 29304, USA

TIMOTHY J. STEER, 62 Stanburn Road, Moortown, Leeds LS17 6NN

JOHN HARVEY VALLENDER, 61 York Close, Bournville, Birmingham B13 0TQ

GAVIN WADELL, Rathlin, Pittville Circus, Cheltenham, Glos GL52 2PX

TONY WALSH, Com Plan Technology Ltd, 7 Milestone Court, Town Street, Stanningley, Leeds LS28 6HE

CLIVE WALTER, Marks & Spencer plc, Michael House, 47–67 Baker Street, London W1A 1DN

PHIL WIGHT, 14 Garendon Road, Shepshed, Leics LE12 9NX

Introduction to Second Edition

WINIFRED ALDRICH

In September 1990 I asked a group of seventy first year textile students beginning HND and Degree courses, 'How many of you have used a computer?' Less than 25% replied 'Yes'. Of this small group only one student had used computer graphics. In October 1993 the same question was put to a similar group of sixty first year students, the percentages had increased, 33% had used a computer and five students had used computer graphics. However, it is apparent that computer literacy is not yet a significant aim in the general education sector.

If students are entering the Higher or Further Education sector as computer illiterates, they should not leave the colleges or universities in the same condition. I believe that the use and discussion of the value of CAD in clothing and textile design is an inseparable part of any current course which is preparing students for a career in either industry or the craft market. There appears to have been an increasing awareness by colleges of the technological changes within the industry. Acceptance of CAD integration can be found in many stated curriculum documents. In practice it can be quite different, there is acute concern about the practical implementation of these aims. This new edition includes a new chapter: 'Teaching Clothing Design by Computer Aided Design: Aspirations and Realities', which discusses these issues.

I am sure that there is still some ignorance about the practical application of CAD and its future potential. This barrier may exist because available knowledge of CAD in clothing and textiles is still sparse. It often has to be sought amongst alien highly technical computer literature which is only marginally useful. Clothing or textile journals are more fertile sources, and some technical books on clothing manufacture offer practical descriptions of processes; but rarely can you find literature that tells you what it is like to work with the technology or that offers well-argued yet sometimes conflicting attitudes towards it.

In this edition many of the contributors have revised or added to their chapters. Current innovations which will affect the industry, particularly in the areas of multi-media and virtual reality, are discussed. Views from the contributors shade from optimistic imminence to a more circumspect position. A philosophical approach by Karen Machin offers a unique, interesting perspective. She opens a discussion that should be of immense interest to anyone concerned with fashion education. I would argue that it is more likely that the users of the technology rather than the software providers perceive the oblique yet crucial design elements of CAD.

Talking about computer aided design is as difficult as talking about the process of design. Discussions of complex concepts, particularly those attempting to describe activities in the visual arts, face communication problems that can only be solved by metaphorical expression. This excites a few and leaves the majority ignorant of the 'idea'. Thus many ideas have a circulatory limit. It is often more useful when searching for the meaning of a word or expression to look at the field in which it is being used. To the participants in that field, use and communication of the word or expression is its 'true' or required meaning at that time. A concept has only a 'true' meaning in the context it is being used; instead of concern about definition, gaining an understanding of the ideas and activities in which CAD is enmeshed would seem to be more fruitful.

My work with student designers given free choice of use of the technology, together with my own personal work, has convinced me that people who say 'CAD is only a tool' have only observed it, or used it in a very limited way, or have rejected it aesthetically or mentally. Such rejections must be respected, but they should not be seen as generalisations. In my research work I found that a student's visual intelligence appeared crucial in their interaction with CAD in the design process, both in competence and means of expression. There were startling contrasts between students who produced immediate realisations of ideas, students who worked structurally, and students who endlessly refined work. When given a choice each student's understanding and use of CAD was different.

I appear, in my work, to exploit the chameleon characteristics of CAD, its amorphous qualities and capacity to be changed and moulded into many different *directed* forms. This is part of its appeal. I am also attracted by the intrinsic quality of the media – glass and light – and I am intrigued by the opportunities to transform a graphic idea on the screen into different forms of output, and by integration with other media. I appear to squander time exploring elements of software with no immediate application; but it is this time that is probably the most valuable. The possibilities are mentally recorded or merged into the software; they may be the *connections* for the design problem that has not yet been conceived. The best solutions often occur when I am engaged on an undemanding but related task – in fact, what appears to be 'messing about'. They come when thoughts are directed away from the problem but still held in some unconscious form. A deadline is often not the problem it would appear to be; in fact, it seems to provide the engine of discovery. Work that is protracted often appears to be inferior.

Observations of the practice of design within the tensions of a commercial environment have shown that CAD need not be a restriction or an unacceptable complication. However, in one's own work there has to be a high degree of personal control over the 'seductive revision' and 'insistent pace' of the technology. But the technology only *offers* alternatives and speed. The selection of work, and a rhythm of work that allows the mind to wander, is a skill; it is knowing 'how' and a resistance to the continual visual prompts. The use of CAD has, in fact, given me more time to work with ideas; it has widened my visual and practical experience; it has given me access to a new medium and to some textile practices that I would have been denied if I had been working manually. I believe that at present CAD has become an integrated part of my process of design. But this is just my personal experience; there are other experiences and other contexts.

A group of people, very knowledgeable, highly respected and working in many fields of CAD, have collaborated in this book to give their perspective of CAD and describe their use of it. Their work covers a wide spectrum: companies who write computer software for clothing and textiles; companies who sell or advise on CAD systems; a CAD bureau; companies who have invested in CAD; designers and technicians using CAD; college lecturers teaching with the technology; and finally some independent views from people who have had varied experiences and interests in the field. The book's contributors should not be seen as some kind of fundamentalist CAD movement seeking conversions; they are simply attempting to dispel some of the mystique or fear that can intimidate or limit a designer's experience of a new phenomenon. It is a phenomenon that, undoubtedly, will have a major effect on design careers in the future.

I would like to thank Kathleen Farrell for the technical index.

THE
SOFTWARE
DEVELOPER

Chapter 1
Writing and Developing Software for CAD Clothing and Textile Systems

STEPHEN GRAY

Stephen Gray, a mathematics graduate, started his career with British Telecom where he gained experience of computer aided design as an executive engineer making printed circuit boards. After eight years with BT (during which time he took a year out to gain a Master's Degree in Computer Science) he moved to an American company, Aydin Controls, where he specialised in producing software for computer graphics applications in the military and power supply industries.

In 1984 he was one of the founder members of Concept II Research, a software company offering low cost systems to the general CAD market. His specialism in the clothing and textiles market grew from a meeting with Winifred Aldrich. Working together with vastly different backgrounds and without funding they demonstrated the potential of cross-disciplinary teamwork by producing ORMUS FASHION.

Stephen Gray is presently Professor of Communications and Computer Graphics at the Nottingham Trent University exploring the potential of Virtual Reality for the fashion industry.

Introduction

Writing good software for any application is difficult – writing for the clothing and textile industry is exceptionally so. Pattern cutters and computer programmers are not natural bedfellows; the former tend to have an artistic background and the latter a scientific one. But collaboration between them can produce really effective software that is powerful in its application and is fun to use. The main challenge of writing for the industry is to appreciate and capitalise on the different perspectives of the computer software writer (programmer) and the user (pattern cutter).

Software is what makes a computer system work. It is sometimes known as a program. In practice software usually means a collection of programs each performing a specific task. Software has to be geared to the industry in which it will be used. To write good software the programmer has to understand the industry, its methods and of course the computer system itself. It is not surprising that the majority of computer applications are in the fields of science and engineering, because many computer experts have backgrounds in the broad scientific subjects and therefore are well placed to provide useful programs to their own community. It is still surprisingly rare to find a programmer with a background of fashion or textile design.

A computer is only as good as its software, and then only as good as the user. Therefore to write software for the clothing industry the author needs to get inside the mind of the pattern cutter or textile designer and understand what tasks they find difficult, boring or time-consuming and identify how a computer system could assist them. A computer system is characterised by the functions that it can perform (e.g. grading or marker making); these are limited by the hardware (e.g. can it cut out cardboard) and are controlled by the software. In writing software for the industry the author therefore has to bear in mind three primary features:

- the functions that the user will require;
- the functions that the hardware can be made to perform;
- the ability of the person who will operate the system.

This final point is extremely important and there are certain broad assumptions that have to be made about the user's knowledge of their craft and his or her ability to use a computer. The computer is no miracle worker and is only a tool in the user's hands. The effectiveness of the tool depends both on its original design and on the way in which it is used.

The remainder of this chapter will concentrate on the pattern cutting side of the business. The comments are equally applicable to textile design applications which can often be simpler to write and comprehend.

A specification

The first task of any software writer is to decide what to do and how to do it. This is a combination of analysis and experience: what tasks does the author wish to perform with the computer system and what practical limitations exist?

The specification of requirements must be written down clearly and comprehensively and must be understandable by both programmer and user. Every possible effort will be made to limit the specification to really useful functions with no frills. Getting these foundations laid down permits future enhancements without altering the original goals. Too often a good idea is ruined because the author lost sight of the original requirements. A good specification provides the basis for the documentation that needs to accompany the system and also for internal notes, test specifications and other support material.

In the clothing and textile industry the majority of software has been written for marker making. The reasons for this are twofold. Firstly, the task is well defined: the aim is to lay down pattern pieces on cloth, minimising the amount of waste material. Secondly, the input and output methods are quickly identified: the user traces in (or digitises) existing pattern shapes which are manipulated on the system and are then output either to a pen plotter to produce a paper marker or directly to a cutting machine.

In writing software for more demanding aspects of the industry (e.g. a pattern design system) the task is more complex and the

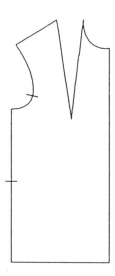

Fig. 1.1. A bodice block with a dart.

creation of a specification becomes more difficult and is more essential. It is important that the specification is created by collaboration between the user and the programmer. One of the fundamental reasons is the different perspective of the computer software writer (or programmer) and the user (pattern cutter). Writing software for this industry is difficult, partly because of the task in hand and partly due to the communication barriers between these two individuals.

The problem is best explained by example, so consider a standard bodice block (Fig. 1.1). There are two very different ways of looking at this and the two have to be married together to produce successful software for the industry.

The pattern cutter's perspective

The block itself gives information about the patterns that it can generate: it has a size (length, width, etc.), a dart, a round neckline and two notches. These features are used by the pattern cutter to make modifications according to personal taste and design objectives. They also show how the piece will be joined to others when the garment is assembled. In addition to the single block pattern there are associated ones (a back, a sleeve, etc.) and changes to one piece frequently dictate the ways in which others can be adjusted.

The computer programmer's view

The block is seen as a series of lines and curves each of which has a measurement. Looking more deeply these can be reduced to a set of co-ordinates that are used to generate the pattern.

The most notable difference between the two perspectives is the meaning associated with the lines on the page. A programmer needs to have the purpose of each explained and then needs to comprehend how each can be used. Consider a standard pattern cutting exercise of 'swinging the dart'; this term makes instant sense to the designer but has to be explained to the computer programmer who would view the operation as a geometric function of moving lines about a fixed point (a standard two-dimensional transformation problem). The operation is shown in Figure 1.2.

This example is one simple exercise in pattern cutting. There are many more in pattern manipulation alone, without considering the requirements of grading and marker making. Going outside the 'normal' pattern operations (for example writing software to per-

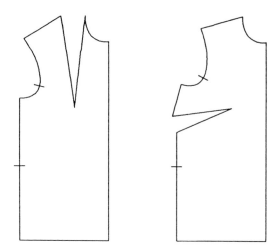

Fig. 1.2. Swinging the dart.

form gathering) vastly extends the required understanding of the programmer.

Another important point in writing the specification is considera-tion of the diversity of the markets into which the software will be sold. The clothing and textile industry is broad, and good, flexible software will have appeal across a wide range of markets. It is worth developing ideas of the ways that the software needs to be written. There are three main sections: the data (or information that needs to be stored); the user functions (the operations that can be applied to this information); and the user interface (or way in which the func-tions are accessed).

The database

Data means the information that needs to be stored on the computer system. In simple terms it means the collection of points, lines and curves that generate the pattern.

Using the same bodice block as in the last section (Fig. 1.1), the computer needs to have a unique way of storing and recalling that shape. The most straightforward way is undoubtedly the best: each pattern piece needs to be stored by a name that both the user and the computer can understand; within that name are stored the points, lines, curves, etc. that comprise the shape. For example the block might be stored in the following format:

Pattern piece name: bodice

Draw a straight line from 5, 5 to 30.5, 5 (the hem)
Draw a straight line from 30.5, 5 to 30.5, 59.85 (the centre front)
Draw a straight line from 5, 5 to 5, 44.1 (The side seam)
Draw a curve from 5, 44.1 through 10.51, 47.54 to 6.25, 60.6 (the sleeve)
Draw a straight line from 6.25, 60.6 to 16.8, 67 (the shoulder)
Draw a straight line from 16.8, 67 to 20.65, 41.6 and another from 20.65, 41.6 to 23.8, 67 (the dart)
Draw a curve from 23.8, 67 to 30.5, 50.85 (the neckline)
Draw a straight line from 3.5, 25.6 to 6.5, 25.6 (the side notch)
Draw a straight line from 9.05, 47.85 to 11.98, 47.23 (the sleeve notch)
End of data

All other pieces can be represented in the same manner, basically a list of instructions or 'recipe' that is used to create the piece to specific dimensions. A whole set of pieces can then be saved together in a file.

This is analogous to manual methods. A file contains individually named pieces (e.g. back, side, etc.) and these pieces are each made up of lines, curves, etc. that join specific co-ordinates together to form the shape. The equivalent manual method is one hanger for a garment containing cardboard templates of pattern pieces each of which is named (e.g. back, side, etc.) and each of which has a specific size.

A computer system is, of necessity, well structured and well organised. It can impose a discipline on a user (e.g. insisting that all pattern pieces are named with precisely six numeric characters) or it can work in harmony with existing manual methods. Poorly written software will impose the discipline and frustrate the user; good software is sympathetic to existing practices. Generally, if the user is well organised before installing a computer system they will have little problem adapting their ways to those of the particular system chosen.

This imposes a strict regime on the software writer though: knowing the ways in which information needs to be retrieved is essential when writing a specification. For example, a pattern cutter thinks of pattern pieces by name (e.g. sleeve) with an overall shape and size, not as a series of lines, curves, notches, etc. linking points together. The programmer needs to organise a method whereby a sleeve can be recalled instantly and where different types of sleeve can be stored without confusion.

A mathematical consideration has to be borne in mind throughout the design of the software: the accuracy of the information that needs to be saved. This has a great effect on the way in which information will be stored and on the speed at which it can be accessed. There is no point in maintaining artificial levels of accuracy, and the pattern cutter will probably be confused if he or she is given measurements to 5 decimal places of accuracy when they normally work to the nearest half a millimetre.

Input, functionality and output

There are three main components to this section: data entry (how information is fed into the system), data manipulation (the operations that are performed on the information) and data output (how the information is extracted from the system).

Input

The input methods are associated with the user interface and indicate the ways in which information (data) will be fed into the machine. It is very important that these are sympathetic to the ways that are well understood by the user and it is the responsibility of the author to understand these methods and provide a computerised version. In the fashion and textile industry it is therefore essential that the programmer understands the artistic basis of many methods used on a day-to-day basis. The input methods must also be compatible with the hardware available, for example the size of a digitiser will limit the size of pattern piece that can be traced into the system.

The specification will identify which method is appropriate and the task of the software writer is to determine how the hardware (e.g. digitising tablet or scanner) will be controlled and how the input information will be read and stored. This is crucial as it affects the way in which data is represented inside the system, which in turn limits how that information can be manipulated and output. The design of the internal data format is usually in the hands of the computer programmer and is rarely fully understood by the user. However, the more the programmer understands about the ways in which the system could be used, the more comprehensive the data base and the more flexible the operations that can be performed on it.

Functionality

The ways in which information is manipulated are really the key to effectiveness of the system: the more powerful the operation the

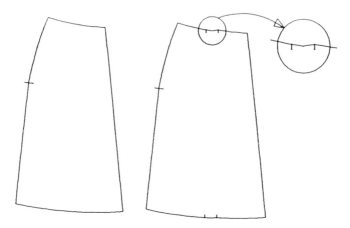

Fig. 1.3. A pleat construction.

more·time that can be saved over and above manual methods. As an example, consider the operations of putting a pleat into a skirt (Fig. 1.3). The first point is the observation of the manual methods (a real challenge for the computer programmer) and then the derivation of the key information that is input to the process.

Following on from this is the analysis of the manipulation that occurs (cutting the pattern, moving it out by the pleat distance and then drawing in the new lines that make up the ends of the pleat). Then comes the difficult bit: writing the software to perform the identical operations with a simple-to-use interface. Implied in this simple description are many important decisions that are not apparent on the surface, for example the direction in which the pleat will be folded, as shown in the ways in which the pleat ends are displayed.

The information that the software will require is:

- position of pleat line;
- pleat distance;
- pleat direction.

It is the task of the software writer to provide these functions in an easy-to-use form.

Output

The computer system is absolutely useless without the ability to obtain something out of it. There are two main methods: hard copy (a print on paper, acetate or similar of the information stored in the system) or direct output to a machine that controls a process such as cutting cloth.

The simplest output is to a pen plotter which draws lines on card or paper. Plotters come in all shapes and sizes: some can take rolls of paper, others only take cut sheets. Some require specialist media and others can take standard pattern cutting cards and papers. The software must be written to control the output device, providing the user with results according to their requirements within the capabilities of the machine.

The whole output process can have its own limitations, for example a machine that cuts with a knife blade needs time to sharpen the edge every so often and the computer programmer may need to build into his software a check to ensure that this happens after the appropriate time. Since each machine has its own characteristics there is often the need to drive several output devices from one piece of software, and this is normally determined by the provision of separate 'device drives' for each type of output machine.

The user interface

Having specified the general requirements of the system there are a number of specific issues that have to be considered. First and foremost is that of the user interface. This term is often misunderstood, but what it really means is how will the user of the system tell the computer what to do next.

Computer systems have many different types of user interface, methods such as pull down menus, pop-up menus, icons, windows, etc. It is the task of the programmer to discuss these with the user and identify the one most suited to the application. There is no golden rule that covers the user interface, other than common sense. The usefulness of individual functions is determined by the ways in which the user interface is presented and these functions should be sympathetic to existing manual practices.

In the example in the last section the functions for making a pleat were outlined; the user interface determines the way in which the user will select the function and input the required information. This will take the form of a selection process: the user must choose to make a pleat and will then respond to various prompts that allow the specific information – pleat distance, direction of fold and precise position – to be input to the system.

Putting it all together

It is essential that the software writer understands the requirements of the market into which the product will be sold. To write effectively he or she needs cross-disciplinary skills: maths, computer science, art, pattern cutting and a bit of engineering too! Since it is rare to find all these skills in one individual it becomes obvious that the only practical way to work is in a small group. In fact good software development implies good teamwork. It is essential that both the 'look' and 'feel' of the software as well as the functionality are right, and this is really only possible when writer and user combine together in a working partnership. But although the emphasis is on teamwork, it is important to realise that there is a supplier/customer relationship: the pattern cutter is the customer while the computer programmer is the supplier.

This perspective may seem one-sided and the question may be asked: 'Why doesn't the pattern cutter need to understand how the computer system works in the same detail?'. There is a strong argument against this. The user needs to understand only the principles of working the system, e.g. data organisation, how to use specific functions, limitations that are imposed by the type of machine, programming considerations or similar; the detail can be regarded as a 'black box'.

Programming decisions such as the choice of computer language or data format are often just confusing. Knowing the reasons why a function is important helps the writer to provide the user with a really effective, easy-to-understand tool. An elementary exercise like measuring along a curve has far reaching and very important implications for the pattern cutter: it is an easy function to write but needs to be presented carefully so that it is easy to use. Adding a seam allowance is a simple function to describe but is very difficult to write since the mathematical formulae depend wholly on the way in which information is stored and used. There are many specific cases that have to be investigated before a general rule emerges. Grading is another function that requires careful study before it can be written correctly.

The conclusion is simple: it is not easy to get it right first time. To create software that is useful, supportable, expandable and hardware-independent requires a mixture of very special talents.

Having written the software there needs to be an intensive period of test, trial and feedback. This too is an essential part of creating a software product and is one that is easy to overlook and push to the background. Once a program has been written it needs to be tested against its original specification: does it do all that was written down and are there any points that were not covered in the original document? After this first level of testing (which is normally performed by the software writer) it needs to be put on trial with a limited number of users who will perform real work and record all the problems that they encounter. This process is known as 'Beta' testing. Their feedback is used to hone the software into a really useful package available to the whole industry. The broader the audience the greater the feedback. The closer the supplier is to the customer the greater the influence of the feedback on future product development and enhancement.

Other considerations

The computer expert also needs to advise the user about the hardware on which it is all to run. This has a major influence on the overall cost of a system to a customer, as well as having a direct relationship to the speed of operations, the amount of information that can be stored and the future expandability of the system.

It should be expected, or even demanded, that the format of data (i.e. the precise detail of the database) is available to all users. Although this information is probably not needed by the user it is a guarantee of independence. The customer needs to ensure that the information he or she creates and stores can be transferred to other systems should the need arise. This facilitates communication between companies and also guarantees that the customer is not tied to one vendor for CAD requirements. Hardware independence is another major consideration; the customer needs to have the right tool for the job and should be specific about the size, speed and quality of the input and output they require. These factors will determine the specific types of hardware.

One of the questions that the software writer must consider, therefore, is that of objectives: is the system to be of general application or is it to be specific to the industry and to the hardware chosen? Nowadays there is absolutely no reason why a system should be tied to specific hardware. There are so many aids to the software writer that the hard work of re-writing for another machine is a simple matter of re-compilation.

There are two obvious choices for the central element of any CAD system (i.e. the computer): the IBM PC compatible machine or the Apple Macintosh. Both have their good and bad points. Although the Macintosh is excellent for desk top publishing it lacks many of the features that make it relevant to the gamut of activities in the clothing and textile industry. Consequently the majority of software in this industry is written for the IBM PC environment. Other options include specialist hardware which is both expensive and inflexible. No computer programmer will choose to limit the hardware on which his or her package will run without very good reason, so software is increasingly becoming available on the standard PC hardware. To help understand the hardware requirements it is worth identifying the elements that make up a system. There are two basic types of CAD system: one for pattern cutting and one for textile design. These are shown in block diagram format in Figures 1.4 and 1.5.

Usually these two functions are divorced from each other: a system can either perform pattern manipulation or it can be used for textile design. To perform both functions separate systems must be purchased because few companies have integrated their pattern cutting and textile design packages. Good software will allow one set of hardware to run both programs.

The author must resist the temptation to provide functions that are a by-product of the technology without thinking about their practical use to the industry. Many poorly written packages are difficult to use and demand an unacceptable knowledge of computer jargon on the part of the user. The application of high technology need not demand the use of high calibre, computer literate users. The software writer must bear in mind the ways in which new users will be trained

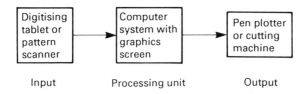

Fig. 1.4. Pattern cutting configuration.

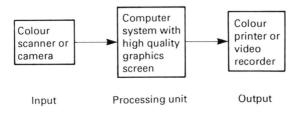

Fig. 1.5. Textile design configuration.

on the system and must always consider their requirements when writing for the industry. The user will find that the computer system needs to be treated as a new medium, similar to but distinct from existing manual methods.

Practical experience

I can only be subjective here and use my own experience in writing the first version of the ORMUS FASHION package. Looking back I can appreciate just how naive I was when I first collaborated on the project with a designer/pattern cutter. I knew nothing about patterns or textiles and had to learn fast. I now think that I know a lot about pattern cutting and after taking art classes at night school have an appreciation of design, but I have never had time to put it all into practice. I understand the ways in which garments are assembled and I am slowly gaining the pattern cutter's eye – namely the ability to look at a shape and criticise it constructively: 'That collar line is wrong and the centre front needs lowering', or even: 'That sleeve will never fit into that bodice; it needs more fullness'. But progress is slow and is really only gained by practical experience. It is what the trainee or apprenticeship schemes used to provide, and something that no vendor can sell: namely experience.

One point that continues to occur though is how much I do not know! As my experience increases I comprehend more and more about the business and identify more and more areas where specialist knowledge exists. To write software for the industry one needs to have a wide range of skills and it is therefore essential to have contacts in all the right places. I have been lucky and have worked extensively with colleges. I have been able to acquire a lot of knowledge by day-to-day contact with students and staff at all levels. Unfortunately, however, there is never time to learn formally the practical and artistic skills necessary to design garments and textiles.

As a supplier of a computer system it is possible to see areas where many companies duplicate work unnecessarily. The division between design and production means that patterns are frequently passed out of the studio and are never seen again by the original designer. The process of grading is frequently done by someone who did not know how the pattern was originally constructed, and therefore mistakes can be made and not picked up until the garment is assembled. An outside eye can provide a wonderfully objective view of where a company can benefit in its working practice, simply by understanding the procedures involved in taking a design right through to production. There are many examples where spin-offs can be made once a CAD system is installed. Consider the process of bra grading: the principles of this process are difficult but once understood they can be used to generate such items as wire charts or lace outline details from the original pattern shapes.

A supplier should work with the customer, building a long-term working relationship to solve problems in all areas of design and production and helping to identify more and more of the areas where CAD technology can add benefits.

The future

Undoubtedly the most exciting and difficult area for the software writer is three-dimensional design. It is still exercising some of the best brains in the world. However, the complexity of specifying their work precludes its acceptance by pattern cutters. The vast number of mathematical calculations involved in making 2D to 3D and making 3D to 2D transformations, (mimicking the ways in which designers work with flat patterns and the dress stand), make it very difficult to operate in a 'user-friendly' manner. Until this barrier is overcome, the usefulness of 3D software will have limited appeal to the pattern cutter.

Conclusion

At first the task looks straightforward, but with increasing knowledge it becomes clear that the task is far more complex than originally imagined. Development takes place in a team comprising a minimum of two experts: the computer programmer who needs to understand manual methods for designing patterns, grading, lay planning and textile design, and the pattern cutter who needs to appreciate the power of the computer system, to understand the principles of data storage and manipulation and who needs to form an analytical approach to his or her work to capitalise fully on a system.

A computer cannot replace a good pattern cutter: it is simply a tool to help them do their job even better. The industry mixes skills from many different areas and CAD technology is just another of these skills. The frustration with writing any software for the industry is that one gains an overall perspective only in retrospect and better approaches to software can usually be identified with the benefit of hindsight. Creating the first version of ORMUS FASHION was highly enjoyable and the product has been successful. It has of course developed significantly since the early days and, like all good software, it continues to grow. This process never stops and good software needs to evolve as new opportunities occur and new technology permits.

Writing software for the clothing and textile industry is exciting and stimulating but very time-consuming. It demands a perpetually open mind and a desire to make art and science work together. The computer programmer can derive enormous satisfaction from writing really useful, time-saving functions and seeing them in use by a creative designer. Working together they can push forward the boundaries of technology as their mutual knowledge increases.

Future for 3D design

It is about three years since I wrote about the ORMUS FASHION system and I included a small section on the future of CAD in the clothing industry. In it I suggested that the subject of 3D design was the greatest challenge to the software writer.

Technology inevitably provides new ideas and the arrival of Virtual Reality heralds the use of truly interactive 3D design tools. The concepts embodied in VR products enable users to control their own position in a 3D 'world' and the use of 3D input devices such as space balls and data gloves is enabling the software writer to build the elementary building blocks necessary for the creation of garments in 3D.

The subject becomes an increasingly complex mixture of art and science with the need to create 3D clothes by joining 2D pattern shapes together. The conceptually simple process of fitting a sleeve into a shoulder is a mathematical nightmare and without a comprehensive understanding of the behavioural characteristics of fabrics the problem remains unsolvable. With the overriding requirement for aesthetic appeal, short cuts and inexactitudes (e.g. add 1 cm for ease) there has to be a compromise between the purity of mathematics and the practicality of construction.

The area of study means that the perennial computer graphics problem of representing 'drape' has to be solved before a viable set of 3D construction tools can be created. There have been significant developments in this field over the last two or three years and the concepts of physically based computer modelling are rapidly gaining credibility and acceptance. These are the basic building blocks required for the clothing design process.

My own work now involves running a research project at the Nottingham Trent University into the use of 2D and 3D tools to create the tools needed to produce the 'computerised fashion show'. The research team comprises a mixture of fashion designers with software writers and clothing production specialists and it hopes to have a product in the market by 1996. The project itself incorporates all the existing tools available in most pattern cutting systems with the graphics packages used to create knitted, woven or printed textiles. The purpose of the link is to produce images that are visually accurate with surface designs scaled to fit on to pattern pieces. The inclusion of physically based modelling techniques is intended to produce dynamic images where mannequins can walk across a computer screen and where the clothes they wear move according to the properties of the materials from which they are made. The addition of VR techniques will permit the user to interact with the 'fashion show', pinning and tucking garments, making design modifications and choreographing their own show.

The subject of 3D remains the future but it is soon to become reality. When it becomes the norm the computer screen will be the next barrier to be removed and perhaps holograms will emerge as the new display medium. After that the industry will turn to the problem of tactile sensation, trying to let users 'feel' fabrics that have yet to be manufactured.

Chapter 2
Software by Design

CAROLINE ASHBY

Caroline Ashby studied Printed Textiles at Chelsea School of Art from 1975–78 before attaining an M.Phil in Constructed Textiles at Middlesex University in 1985.

She became involved with CAD in 1985, and continued active involvement in its use and development, working in an advisory capacity, as well as doing freelance designing and lecturing. From 1989–1992 she worked as Textile Systems Manager for a computer software product Cameo Paint. In 1993 she formed her own company, CAD for CAD, Caroline Ashby Designs, to launch Eneas Designer and to address the specific needs of the design and pre-production process for the clothing and textile industry, together with training and consultancy services.

Introduction

Cast your mind back to your first glimpse of 'painting with light' on a Computer Aided Design terminal. Where were you? What were you doing there? What were your first thoughts about this new phenomenon? Did it thrill you? Excite you? Interest you? Or did you think merely that it was just another electronic gadget to clutter our technological age – that it would not catch on?

Did you stop to wonder how it was possible to copy an image so quickly, to flip it, rotate it, fill it with brilliant translucent colours, all within seconds? Did you wonder how this so-called computer came to work like this? Did you ever wonder how the program was compiled, and who was delegated to create an acceptable aid to assist the design process?

To the layman, software is perhaps seen as a computer 'buzz' word and many may not know its true significance. In computer terms it describes a highly intricate mathematical process which, when packaged as a finished program, provides the user with a powerful means of control for completing a specific task quickly and effectively. The 'blood in the veins' is perhaps an apt definition.

As a designer, trained traditionally in both printed and woven textiles, I have found it of immense interest and a great opportunity to be involved in the forefront of software development for CAD systems for the clothing and textile industries. This chapter is based on personal experience and observation, supported by much detailed information from colleagues – the computer experts as well as fellow designers. It is intended to provide an insight into the technical intricacies and parameters of using CAD in these industries, not only to aid current CAD users but also to provide inspiration to others who are interested or may benefit from becoming involved.

Many traditionally trained designers still hesitate to use CAD wholeheartedly, in the way they would naturally pick up a crayon or paintbrush. Over the years they have tended to respond in a number of different ways to the idea of freely using CAD. Some cannot wait to get started, sensing immediately that here is a tool to really assist the daily design routines. Probably the majority are intrigued by the idea but their interest goes no further, often simply because an affordable design system is not available for training for any length of time. Many disbelieve that a computer can actually aid the design process at all, and indeed some completely reject the idea with such views as: 'Computers are machines in boxes and have nothing to do with design or artists' materials, and anyway I am a designer and I do not need a computer'. End of story.

This last response appears to come most from the older generation who frequently say that they are too old to learn about computers.

Naturally, within all these groups there are exceptions to the rule, and importantly there is a small, growing sector encompassing a cross-section of professional activity and age, who can be seen as the clothing and textile CAD pioneers, seriously committed to the future development and implementation of CAD within these industries.

From a software engineering viewpoint, limited understanding of the traditional design processes as well as the specific market areas – be it clothing, printed or constructed textiles or embroidery – can often create a gulf in communication between computer technologist and designer and/or production technician, causing a somewhat restrictive software program to result. Limited funds for research and development can also be a cause of this, together with a simple lack of specific development policies within the large software organisations.

To provide the type of specialist design software required by the users within these different market sectors, a close union must be formed between software engineer and design and production specialist, since the ultimate success of the program is dependent on effective communication in the development stages. The software and hardware companies must be well informed on the specific design and manufacturing requirements of the textile and clothing industries so that they are able to provide the customer with the most up-to-date and effective product, along with reliable support and training.

This chapter will illustrate, in designer terms, some of the major computer considerations, software or hardware, and advantages or disadvantages to the design process, of which CAD users should be aware. It is hoped that identification of what the computer can and cannot do from a technical viewpoint, will provide a basis from which the CAD user can become more familiar with the true capabilities of such a sophisticated tool, so that some of the mystery, and in some cases fear, which continues to exist, can be overcome. Once this is achieved, designers can start to push the technology to its creative limit, hitherto unseen to any degree, which in turn is likely to influence the type of design imagery seen in the 21st century.

Technical parameters

After examining some general computer technicalities, this chapter follows the design process, i.e. conceptualisation, manipulation and production. It is intended to provide the CAD user with a simple means of reference.

Figure 2.1 illustrates a personal computer (PC) design system featuring typical hardware technology: a scanner, computer, 14 in text monitor, keyboard, digitising tablet, 19 in colour monitor and colour printer, all of which enables the designer to complete the design process electronically.

The computer

Probably the one component more shrouded in mystery to the designer than any other is the computer itself, which can be seen as the nerve centre. Without it, all other components remain inoperative. A valuable exercise for any user is to see inside the computer box, to gain an idea of the basic workings.

Fig. 2.1. A PC-based design system.

Inside every graphics design system is a particular type of so-called graphics board, usually a rectangular circuit board covered in electronic bits and pieces, known as chips and processors and the like. Depending on the make of design system used, a graphics board can be slotted in and removed as simply as loading or unloading a plate from a dishwasher. Graphics boards have to be treated with respect; they are costly and form a vital, integral component on which the software is run. Today it is possible to buy not only standardised graphics boards, manufactured by the computer giants, but also custom-built graphics boards from specialist hardware manufacturers.

The other major components within the computer are:

(1) the central processor unit which effectively operates software programmes; it fetches, decodes and executes instructions through active RAM memory;
(2) the storage memory, into which information can be inserted and stored for future use on a hard disk inside the computer or on floppy disk (either 5.25 in or 3.5 in);
(3) the input and output lines to enable information to be taken in and out of the system, such as from scanners, or to printers;
(4) the power supply.

Monitors

The monitor is the display screen for seeing either data or graphics. Some design systems require only one monitor, others two, depending on the complexity of the software program and the particular graphics board being used. Monitors are made up of thousands of tiny dots, through which the graphic imagery is displayed by means of 'pixels' or 'picture elements', which on the graphics screen is the smallest element to be seen and controlled individually. Monitors vary as to the resolution – the total number of pixels which can be seen over the entire screen at once. Therefore the more pixels your monitor can handle the better the design imagery will look, providing the graphics board is compatible in terms of resolution.

Every addressable dot on the screen is numbered for convenience, and an important point is that software must be written to run on a rectangular shaped screen, which in itself is a technical parameter. Monitors are seen in the computer trade as being at a 4 to 3 aspect ratio, which can cause limitations from a mathematical viewpoint.

The colour image is made up of a combination of three basic colours: 'red-green-blue', or R,G,B as it is known. Inside every monitor are three electron guns, each of which handles the production of one colour.

There are two methods of refreshing colour screens, known as interlaced and non-interlaced. Interlaced displays first the even lines of visual data from the top to the bottom of the monitor, followed by the uneven lines. Hence only half the visual data is seen at one time and is usually displayed at a rate of 25 times per second. The visual effect is that the screen image is shimmering slightly, identical to any television picture seen today.

Non-interlaced operates by displaying each line of visual data in turn, from top to bottom, refreshing the whole screen at a rate of 50–90 times per second. The impression is that the image is completely still and unaffected by any flickering. Naturally this type of flicker-free non-interlaced graphics board and colour monitor is far more suitable for design work.

Monitors are measured diagonally across the screen to determine the working dimension, and vary in size from 12 inches upwards. In general terms, the larger the display area the easier it is for the designer to visualise creatively, as this provides a closer simulation to the traditional working environment.

Digitising tablets

The digitising tablet is the device which helps the designer create and edit the design on the monitor, and consists of a flat board which is positioned in front of the monitor and attached to the computer with a cable. Each tablet is accompanied by a pen, or a puck – a device incorporating a cross within a glass sight, with a number of function buttons. Some design systems support the use of a 'mouse' rather than a tablet but from a design viewpoint a pen is preferable to the mouse or puck, since it emulates the designer's traditional tool kit.

Most tablets vary in size from around A5 to A3, or even larger which can be useful if artwork is to be traced on to the system via the tablet. The 'active' workable area is not necessarily the whole area of the tablet, and often it takes designers a little time to gain precise control of this aspect.

Accompanying pens vary also, and it is worth testing different types since the right 'feel' aids design performance. Some pens tend to be rather insensitive and seem to need more pressure to activate them. Conversely, some are ultra sensitive. Some pens are attached to the digitising tablets via a flex, and some are cordless. There are also pressure sensitive pens which give the designer a little more creative freedom.

The keyboard

The use of the keyboard to aid the design process can be most beneficial, since many commands can be controlled by individual keyboard letters, enabling the task to be completed more quickly than using complicated sequences of pen movements. Most design systems running their own specialised software use the keyboard to activate functions within the paint program, in their own unique manner. For example, to select the whole screen area using Eneas Designer software, the designer can actually place a rectangle around the whole screen area, or press A for 'ALL' on the keyboard, which is quicker.

In addition, the keyboard is naturally a vital tool when creating text within the paint program as part of the design process, for example, for casualwear placement prints or for saving images quickly to hard or floppy disk, for storage. Hence the keyboard should be viewed as an aid to the design process, and not just as part of a 'typewriter'.

Resolution

Probably one of the most difficult areas to understand when starting to use CAD is resolution. This describes the number of addressable points which can be represented visually and is termed 'dots per inch', relating to the number of dots measured over an inch in the same way as the unit measurement for structuring woven textiles is warp ends and weft picks per inch or centimetre.

Every hardware component along the design process generally supports a different resolution, or dpi (dots per inch) as it is known. Colour scanners read visual images at a maximum of 300 or 400 dpi. Graphics boards support varying resolutions depending on the particular type of board. The resulting dpi seen on screen by the designer varies according to the size of the monitor.

Table 2.1 identifies some current personal computer graphics boards, their onscreen resolution, example monitor sizes, and the resulting dpi seen by the designer. The figures for onscreen resolution (640 × 480 for example) represent the total number of dots or pixels seen across and down the monitor.

In computing terms the width and depth of the screen are known as the X and Y axes respectively and represent the columns and rows of pixels which make up the whole screen. Since each pixel can be addressed separately, each has an X and Y position on the screen which acts as a guide for the software engineer as the program is written. Hence the higher the resolution, the finer the image quality will be on screen.

Table 2.1. Common resolution variables.

Graphics board	Onscreen resolution	Monitor size (in)	DPI (approx.)
Standard VGA	320 × 200	15	24
Enhanced VGA	640 × 480	15	50
Super VGA	800 × 600	15	65
Video display (broadcast)	768 × 576	15	64
High resolution	1024 × 768	19	70
	1280 × 1024	19	90
	1600 × 1200	19	112
	2048 × 2048	19	166

A further resolution variable is that every colour printer available on the market today prints out at a specific dpi. For example, some print at 160 dpi while others print at 300 dpi, using perhaps a maximum of 8 colours combined in such a way as to produce a range of hundreds or thousands of further colours. The total number of colours which can be produced from different printers varies according to the particular printing method used. An immense number of variables exist, therefore, with each hardware component, which in turn controls the manner in which the image has to be produced – a technical parameter.

It might be suggested that all hardware should be standardised to a specific dpi, but this in itself would create enormous creative restrictions and in addition would put many hardware companies out of business. Furthermore, input and output devices such as scanners and printers are not restricted to textile and clothing use alone but are employed across the spectrum of business activities.

General software terms

In support of the hardware identified above, there are general software terms and operations which aid a designer's understanding.

User interface

From a software viewpoint the user interface describes the manner of control of a software program by the user. In general, software programs are provided with a standard operations procedure, usually displayed in the form of a series of menus or lists which allow the user to select a specific function to complete a particular task.

The visual appearance of the user interface varies considerably with different design systems (see Fig. 2.2), but the principles of control are the same, allowing the user to activate the various software routines. There is a current trend for many software programs to be operated by means of pop-down menus, accompanied by icons or symbols representing the function's action. For example, to fill an area of an image with colour, the icon displaying a paint pot is selected. This type of user interface is standard to all Apple Macintosh technology. More specialist paint programs are operated by user interfaces individual to the particular software company specifications, and will vary.

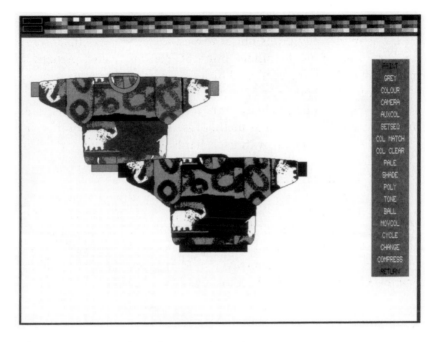

Fig. 2.2. User interface showing the colour palette and menu of Eneas Designer (courtesy of Eneas Informatica S.R.L.).

Rasters and vectors

Images can be displayed on screen in two fundamental ways: a raster or vector display.

From a design viewpoint it is important to understand the differences, and the benefits and restrictions of each, otherwise confusion and frustration can result because certain creative operations are difficult or impossible using one or other type of display. All CAD systems are referred to as raster based or vector based, and to the layman the differences are simple.

Rasters

Raster images are displayed on screen as a series of dots or pixels. Each pixel can be lit up independently from as few as 256 simultaneous colours to a maximum of a few million on screen at any one time, enabling complex, high quality multicoloured imagery to be achieved when displayed on higher resolution monitors.

Vectors

Vector images comprise lit vectors or 'line segments', which when joined together form fine quality smooth lines, often displayed in one colour only. Outline shapes can be created very simply, each made up of a number of control points which can be manipulated easily and effectively to alter the image.

Essentially therefore, every shape created becomes an independent component part made up of a number of control points, as Figure 2.3 shows. Subsequently the component parts can be filled with solid colour.

Table 2.2 identifies both the major benefits and restrictions to the designer of these two display types. At a glance it is possible to see that the raster based display is technically more advanced for the input, manipulation, and subsequent output of a wide range of visual imagery, which can be simple or complex. This is because the images are made up of tiny multi-coloured dots, providing the designer with flexible 'painting' facilities and allowing a considerable amount of freedom for visual. creation.

Naturally there are restrictions, the major one being that the edges of the imagery are distinctly 'jagged', like a series of stepped blocks, when seen on a lower resolution monitor or output from certain

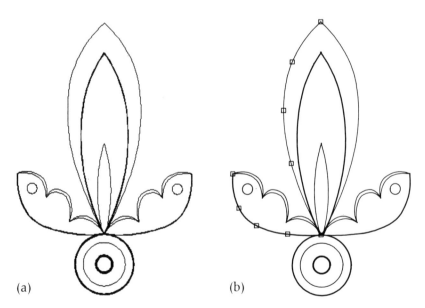

(a)   (b)

Fig. 2.3. Visual differences of a line image drawn on (a) a raster based system, (b) a vector based system.

Table 2.2. Major benefits and restrictions of raster and vector displays.

Display type	Visual representation	Benefits	Restrictions
Raster	● (pixel)	Images can be complex and highly coloured. Between 256 and 1.5 million colours can be seen on screen at one time. Extensive range of 'painting' functions possible, e.g. colour enhancing, cutting and pasting, soft airbrushing. Good for scanning and cleaning up scanned images, and image capture from camera or video input. Full control over each pixel on monitor.	At lower resolutions image outlines are shown as jagged or stepped. Fine outlines can break up when scaling image.
Vector	▬ (line segment)	Efficient at drafting, measuring, and scaling outlines. High quality printed and plotted results. Easy manipulation and layering of images.	Usually only up to 256 colours available. Very limited 'painting' facilities. Unable to scan in and clean up scanned images, unless very simple.

colour printers. Where fine smooth lines are an integral part of the design, achieving an acceptable visual quality without 'jaggies' can be difficult. Solving this problem means going to much higher resolutions or dpi on the monitor, so that the irregularity of the outline becomes mainly indistinguishable to the eye. The drawback of this is that higher resolutions cost more money.

Vectors, on the other hand, are made up of 'line segments' and so provide more limited painting and colouring facilities, but the creation and manipulation of outlines can be achieved more easily. Therefore vector software is used extensively for lay planning and grading, as well as the final stages of embroidery design.

Figure 2.3 illustrates diagrammatically the visual differences of lines on a raster based and vector based system. At the moment raster and vector displays are incompatible from a software point of view, being difficult to work together technologically. Sometimes even established CAD users have not been aware of the differences of the two techniques, and have been puzzled as to why, for example, outlines on raster based systems can lose some detail when scaled to a different size. However, on some systems this has been compensated by the development of software routines which improve the quality of line images in raster based systems.

Operating systems

Every computer has a disk operating system, which essentially consists of a special software program to ensure that the system as a whole operates in a correct and orderly fashion, ensuring the simple listing, saving, recalling and running of programs. It may be seen as a behind-the-scenes 'personal organiser'.

Many personal computers today run an operating system known as MS-DOS which stands for Microsoft's Disk Operating System. The more powerful, sophisticated computers known as workstations run other types of operating systems, such as Unix, providing additional benefits not readily available with a personal computer.

Some personal computers, such as the Apple Macintosh range particularly, hide the operating system from the user by covering it completely with a graphical user interface. For most designers this is desirable, since involvement with MS-DOS can be an intimidating experience – visually it looks like double Dutch! Generally it is not necessary for the designer to become too involved with DOS but knowledge of its existence is useful and aids general understanding by allowing the designer to get more from the system.

Apart from being a command structure, MS-DOS is the software engineer's entrance to accessing the computer, to add or alter software operations. If involvement with DOS is necessary for any reason, the main point to remember is *don't panic*! You will survive, and so will the computer! Essentially the operating procedure is straightforward and logical, and although it does take a little time to understand operations, it can be seen as identical to keeping a loose-leaf file of information split into various sections or directories.

System crashes

A colloquial computer term heard every so often is 'the system crashed'. This means that for some reason the software program has jammed or stuck, disabling operations totally. This is quite likely to happen to a CAD user, as the result of a number of different possible causes, for example: selecting an odd sequence of functions; not properly selecting a function; not enough disk space or memory; or occasionally it may be a hardware fault, such as power supply fatigue.

When the system crashes, again *don't panic*! You will not have broken the whole machine but just stalled it, similar to stalling a car. To continue working, the system will have to be restarted, or re-booted as it is known technically.

If the system does crash during work, and the design has not already been saved in the library, that particular piece of work might be lost depending on the particular type of graphics board being used in the machine. Therefore it is important to adopt the habit, when starting to use a design system, of periodically saving the design while working on it, so that if the machine crashes a recent version of the image can be retrieved immediately from files after rebooting, so saving the designer from having to start again.

Scanning

Desktop scanners, as opposed to the larger drum scanners used by the printing industry, are available in a number of different sizes. The smallest is an A5 handheld version, A4 is a medium size, and A3 is the largest size for the average budget, in keeping with a PC based system. Naturally, for inputting a wide range of visual imagery a colour scanner is more desirable than black and white, although the latter is perfectly acceptable.

The software enables images to be scanned at various dpi (dots per inch) according to the task being carried out. Currently the general parameters for scanning on a personal computer are 35 dpi minimum, and 400 dpi maximum, with a number of possible variations in between. Any part of an image can be selected for scanning, and it is important to be aware of three main factors:

(1) The process of scanning requires a certain amount of disk space to operate, so the computer's hard disk space should be checked before scanning starts. The higher the resolution selected the more disk space required for scanning.

(a)

(b)

Fig. 2.4. Size and visual difference of an image scanned at (a) 75 dpi, (b) 300 dpi.

(2) The particular dpi selected for scanning will govern the resulting size of the image. If an image scanned at 100 dpi is compared with an image scanned at 200 dpi, the higher resolution image will be four times larger in size overall, and more detailed simply because more dots or pixels are used. Therefore if a high quality scan is required, a higher resolution should be selected. Figure 2.4 shows the difference in size and detail of the same image scanned at 75 dpi and 300 dpi.

(3) After scanning, the image will consist of multiple colours irrespective of how many colours there are on the original artwork.

(a)

(b)

Fig. 2.5. Magnified section of art work showing colour content (a) original artwork, (b) after scanning, (c) after cleaning up.

To convert the scanned picture to the same number of colours as the original, colour compression software must be used. Some paint programs provide this, some do not. If not, the artwork must be cleaned of all rogue colours by hand which can take many hours of laborious work. Figure 2.5 illustrates the colour differences of a magnified section of artwork before and after scanning, and after cleaning up the image using colour compression software.

Colour

Colour palettes, and the possibilities for manipulating and controlling colour on raster based design systems, are infinite and complex. They result from binary arithmetic, on which digital computing is based. On the higher resolution raster based CAD systems it is possible to access between 262 000 and 16.7 million colours for design use, with between 256 and 1.3 million colours on screen simultaneously, depending on the graphics board and the size of monitor.

These figures are standard and depend on a number of technical parameters. Without going into too much mathematical detail, the particular graphics board used in the system will consist of a particular number of bits-per-pixel. A bit is the smallest unit of binary information stored in the computer, and a group of 8 bits – a BYTE – is capable of storing one of 256 possible functional alternatives.

Graphics boards are made to support a number of different bits-per-pixel, all of which are multiples of four. For example:

- 8 bits-per-pixel
- 12 bits-per-pixel
- 16 bits-per-pixel
- 24 bits-per-pixel
- 32 bits-per-pixel

Generally personal computer design systems use graphics boards which are either 8 bit, 24 bit or less commonly 32 bit. How these technicalities control colour, and subsequently affect the designer, can be explained simply.

Design system working in 24 bit mode

Red, green and blue are the primary colours associated with the additive colour process, and as mentioned previously a group of 8 bits allows 256 alternatives. Since every dot or pixel on screen can be addressed separately, working in 24 bit mode essentially means that every dot can have 256 different levels of firstly red, secondly green, and thirdly blue, making a total available palette of 16 777 216 different colours. It should be noted that on a 19 in monitor displaying 1280 × 1024 pixels, only about 1.3 million colours can be seen at once.

Design system working in 8 bit mode

The mathematical restrictions of colour working in 8 bit mode can be confusing for the designer, so only the very basic principles are explained here.

Although the maximum number of colours is again 16.7 million, only 256 colours can be handled at any one time. The translation of colours from computer to monitor occurs in what is called the look-up table or LUT. On an 8 bit system, each pixel contains a number between 0 and 255. This number points to an entry in the LUT, which in turn gives three values between 0 and 255 for the red, green and blue component of the required colour. Since there are 256 entries in the LUT, each pixel can be defined as any one of 256 × 3 colours, giving a total of 16.7 million.

How does this affect the designer? Table 2.3 lists the main creative advantages and disadvantages of working in the different modes.

A further important factor regarding colour is the understanding of the two fundamental colour processes. Obtaining colours by mixing rays of light, as on a computer, is known as the 'additive' colour process, whereas mixing pigments or dyes to obtain colours is known as the 'subtractive' colour process.

Here we have one of the most difficult dilemmas of CAD: it is technologically impossible at this time to reproduce the colours available on a computer on a sheet of paper, and vice versa, because of the fundamental differences between the two colour processes. Much research has been, and continues to be, undertaken in an attempt to overcome this technical difficulty, but a further problem is that it is very easy to adjust the brightness and contrast of the monitor from day to day, thus affecting the colours seen on screen.

Figure 2.6 illustrates the rudimentary differences and distribution of additive and subtractive colours.

Table 2.3. Advantages and disadvantages of 24 bits *v* 8 bits-per-pixel

	Advantages	Disadvantages
24 bit	Maximum number of colours available.	Unable to flood fill areas of imagery quickly.
	Good for airbrush, wash, shade, tint, softening the edges of a raster image by averaging the intensity of neighbouring pixels, and colour mixing, i.e. for creating more subtle visual effects.	Unable to create colourways easily. Disk space can fill up quickly. Loading full screen pictures can be slow without a dedicated hard disk.
	Good at merging complex images.	
	Excellent quality visual results for presentation.	
8 bit	Quick colour manipulation such as flood fill and creating colourways.	Only 256 colours on screen at once.
	Only 256 colours on screen at once (fewer colours on screen at once could be seen as an advantage).	Special functions and features such as airbrushing and merging images are limited or not possible.
		Sometimes a striped effect occurs when scanning subtly shaded images.
		Unable to display multiple designs on one screen using different colour palettes for each. Not enough colours.

Colour printers

A convenient point to consider initially is how to colour match the image on screen so that it can be correctly printed on to the paper. A number of possibilities are available, none of them totally satisfactory:

• Each printer is able to produce a certain number of colours which will vary according to the particular technology. Either the colours can be matched automatically by the computer to the particular printer, or the designer does it by means of a colour book which relates to the colours available.

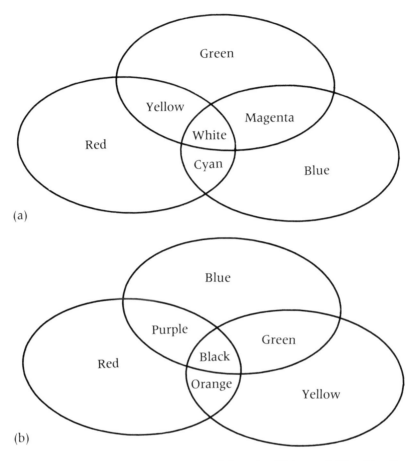

Fig. 2.6. Differences and distribution of the (a) additive and (b) subtractive colour process.

- Some design systems support specific production colour systems such as Pantone and Scotdic, which provide not only a colour chart but a reference number for each colour. As yet it is not possible to output these colours automatically from any printer.
- Some printers attempt to colour match as accurately as possible without the designer having to resort to controlling the colour. If the colours are simple primaries or brights sometimes the results are acceptable, but it can be rather hit and miss.
- Colours available from the printer will vary with the particular manner in which the dots are printed on to the paper. There are various printing alternatives, known technically as 'dither patterns' and 'microfont matrices', which essentially control the pattern and

the number of dots printed. For example, one pixel on screen maps to 4 dots horizontally and vertically on the printer. This is known as a 4 × 4 microfont matrix size. There are various microfont sizes and by altering these it is possible to manipulate the total number of colours a printer is able to produce. The resulting visual effects of imagery printed with different microfont matrices can be a useful aesthetic aid to the designer.

There are a variety of printers on the market today, all operating different processes. These include ink-jet, thermal, dot matrix, laser and, more recently, sublimation. Prices range from £600 to £60 000.

Paper surface and size will vary with each printer, being either shiny or matt and ranging generally from A5 to A3. A £60 000 printer can print up to between A1 and A2 in size and is matt.

Library storage

One of the most beneficial aspects of a CAD system is the ability to store designs, images, text or whatever within the library. The saving and retrieval of designs is a simple operation which generally takes a few seconds, depending on the size and complexity of the visual.

As CAD becomes more common in the textile and clothing sectors, and as CD-ROM technology advances, companies are beginning to realise the potential of retaining a visual database of designs in this media rather than in cardboard boxes which are left to gather dust in a warehouse. With CAD, designers have at their fingertips all the resource material required for developing future design ranges.

A software engineer's view

Generally when a new piece of software is to be written, there is a typical procedure followed by the engineer to create the program. (The word 'create' has been used deliberately since software writing is a creative activity.)

Initially the engineer will determine the purpose of the function – What is it supposed to do? This is followed by determining how to present the user interface for the designer so that it works fluently and effectively. At this point the basic options of the function are worked out, followed by the primitive operations to get the function working; for example the menu colours on screen and a simple toolkit which might consist of adding in some numbers or a few questions and answers.

It is then possible to start building the function by looking at the basic operations, for example 'In > Option > Out', and trying out each option of the function one by one. The aim is to check that all options available to the designer integrate well together and provide the most direct manner of achieving the solution.

Ninety per cent of the program takes 10% of the time to write, and the final 10% takes 90% of the time to test and perfect. As with

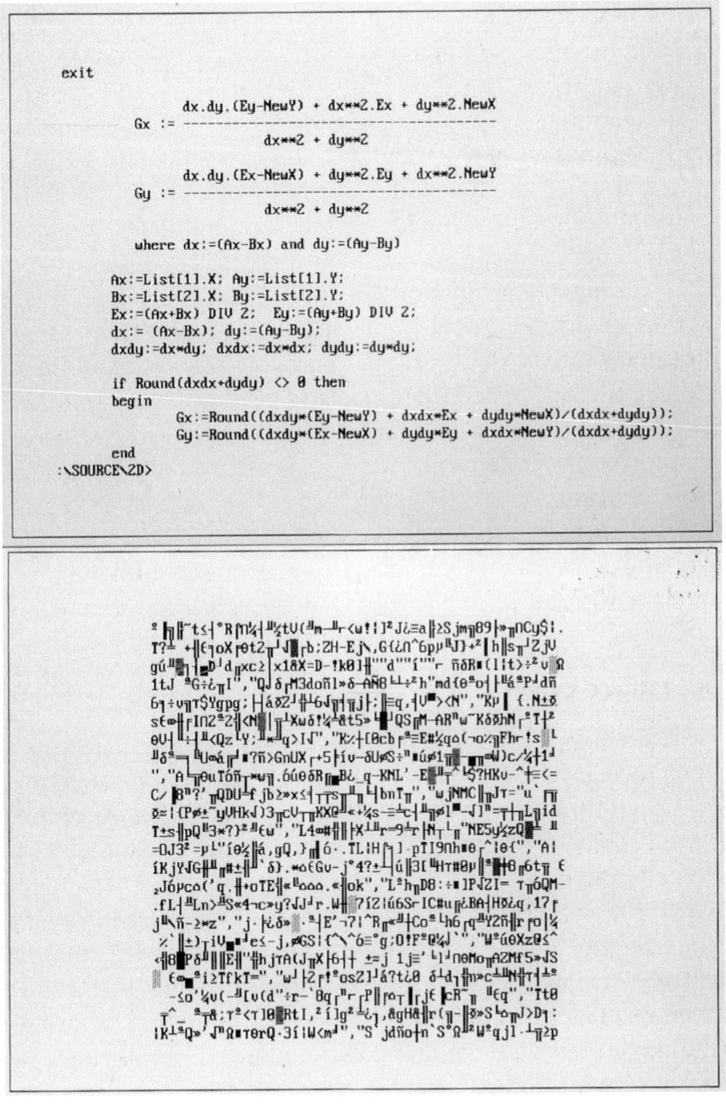

(a)

(b)

Fig. 2.7. The visual appearance of (a) software code, (b) computer trash.

designers, software engineers have their own handwriting which can be identified by other programmers as different methods of arrangement and the amount of attention paid to getting the function or program to operate efficiently.

The visual composition of software code on screen comprises a mixture of letters, symbols and sentences, as shown in Figure 2.7.

From a designer's viewpoint, working closely with a technical team can provide a fascinating insight into software development and can facilitate a more realistic understanding of the technical parameters which govern CAD.

Summary

Once a designer has had the opportunity of working on a CAD system and has sampled the magic, for example, of colouring a design in a fraction of the time it would have taken traditionally, the immediate response is to expect the system to do every task that needs to be done, and as quickly. Unfortunately this is not possible.

This chapter has brought to the attention of CAD users some of the basic parameters of what can and cannot be achieved and the reasons why. In turn it is hoped that designers of the present and the future will be encouraged to become more involved and will take more interest in learning about the basic technicalities of this most exciting design tool.

Many times in the past few years designers have been heard to remark, 'I don't want to know anything about computers; I just want it to work without getting involved in the technical side'. This can be understood, but such a view is limiting since with any machine there is a certain amount the user has to know in order to operate it effectively. For instance, a car is a reasonably sophisticated machine which the driver must first learn to operate, before passing a test to indicate a degree of skill and competence. With continued practice it is possible for the driver to fine-tune driving performance, and subsequently the driver must learn to maintain the car so that it operates to its full potential.

Naturally a designer does not have to take a test in order to use CAD, but there is a certain amount of learning with regard to the particular computer and software package which can include some technical understanding, but no more so than that of driving and maintaining a car. By so doing the designer is in a much stronger position to gain the real benefits of working with such an advanced tool.

There is also a need for the computer experts, be they research and development or sales based, to listen seriously to the requirements of the clothing and textile industries, particularly regarding design and production software. All too often in the past the computer companies have dictated to designers as to their requirements, without truly understanding design tasks. This inevitably causes confusion and frustration to the user since they are being asked to think and operate in an alien manner. It would appear that some computer companies expect designers to adjust their working habits substantially to fit in with the software package.

When suggestions have been made by designers for specific functions, a regular response from technical departments has been 'Why do you want to do this?', followed by 'It cannot be done'. As a result, all too often, the newly purchased system is left to sit in a room by itself, untouched, since it is not sympathetic to a designer's manner of working.

For the producers and users of CAD technology to push out the barriers and break new ground, both technologically and aesthetically, *both* sectors must become more aware of the other's requirements and technical parameters, rather than each sitting in ivory towers. A more integrated working relationship than has so far taken place between CAD producer and user, must provide a better foundation for continued computerised development to assist the clothing and textile industries in the future.

Acknowledgement

All Registered Trademarks are acknowledged including Microsoft Corporation, Apple Computer Ltd, Pantone Inc., Scott-Munsell Colour System, Eneas Informatica S.R.L.

THE MARKETER

Chapter 3
Marketing CAD/CAM

DOUGLAS COOPER AND TIM STEER

Douglas Cooper was educated in South Africa. He spent five years working in clothing manufacture, five years in production and two years in sales. He then entered the family textile machinery business where he worked for many years.

For thirteen years he was involved in the introduction, sales and the servicing of CAD/CAM equipment in the United Kingdom. His experience and knowledge of the early introduction of CAD/CAM into large companies was gained by his practical involvement in major CAD installations. He has now retired and lives in South Africa.

Tim Steer has been involved in sales and support worldwide since 1987. During that time he has engineered the integration of CAD/CAM systems into many respected apparel and furniture industry companies.

THE HISTORICAL BACKGROUND OF CAD/CAM

DOUGLAS COOPER

CAD/CAM systems

The history of CAD/CAM clothing systems is a complex tale centred on the appearance (and disappearance) of various suppliers of CAD/CAM equipment to the garment industry.

It was in the early 1970s that four men in Dallas, Texas, got together and thought about the idea of making markers on a computer. This was the foundation of CAMSCO. At that time operators who made markers manually were having to travel backwards and forwards along long laying-up tables, placing card pattern pieces on paper and drawing round them. If one thinks about the different sizes and pieces involved, the gap between the pieces, the constraints (e.g. nap, flip, tilt, etc.) one can appreciate that it was no easy job. Above all else the marker had to be efficient, i.e. giving the best possible fabric yield.

The ability to computerise the placing of pieces within a given area was not such a difficult task. The real difficulty was that these pieces were odd shapes which contained punch holes, notches, stripe lines, grain lines etc. and these all had to be catered for by the computer system. This problem was solved by electronically tracing the irregular shapes and related information and feeding this data into the computer – a function referred to as digitising, and this worked very well.

There was one other task which these four men from Dallas wanted to achieve and that was the ability to grade via the computer. To grade manually was a long-winded process because new pattern pieces had to be made for each size. It was decided that grade-rule tables should be created. This meant that the X and Y directional co-ordinates for a grade point were assigned a rule number. To generate the same movement for another grade point it would only be necessary to apply the corresponding number. With this in hand they now had the basis for a grading and marker making system. The output of graded pieces, singularly or nested, as well as planned markers, either scaled down or full size, was possible by the use of a plotter made by Gerber, another American company.

Just after the Dallas team set to work, another software house in America acquired the expertise of two of the Dallas programmers and started to develop their own system which they marketed for three or four years under the name of The Hughes AM1 System. Eventually this system was sold to Gerber, who had already established themselves as suppliers of plotters and numerically controlled (NC) cutting equipment.

By this time there were two US companies supplying marking and grading systems. Both established offices in Europe and England (I headed up one of them). While all this had been going on, a Spanish clothing manufacturer had been developing a system for in-house use, but they did not enter the selling arena until the late 1970s or early 1980s. It is interesting to note that all three companies were using Hewlett Packard mini computers as the platform for their software, and the results were good. At this time PCs had not come into their own.

Later in the 1980s a French company, Lectra, started developing their system, so we now had four companies marketing computerised marking and grading. It was not long after this that Gerber bought CAMSCO and founded the Gerber Camsco Organization; so we were back to three companies. Five years later Ron Martell, who had been one of the Dallas four, started his own company, Microdynamics, and brought out a PC based system.

The development of the Assyst system

Around the same time Assyst, a team of four in Germany who had worked for the US companies as well as the Spanish company, were listening to the market. As they were maintaining many systems throughout Europe they had established relationships with many manufacturers. There was a 'hole' in the market place for a pattern design system. Although all the competitive systems suppliers at that time were offering pattern design and/or manipulation facilities on their equipment to varying degrees, none were satisfying the market at large which had an appetite for a pattern design system (PDS) which could successfully be used in a production environment.

Numerous manufacturers discussed this problem with Assyst, who decided to write such a package. The company had a good working knowledge of systems on the market and they were able to note down, in their plans for a new system, the good and bad points of existing systems in the market place and what was needed. In addition, they had at their disposal much more powerful hardware and more sophisticated software development tools to choose from than CAMSCO or Gerber ever had at their outset. They also had the choice of whether to go for a PC based system, as the others in the field were doing, or to go the mini computer route. They chose the Hewlett Packard mini computer route for many reasons.

Their first task was to develop a PDS which could be used in a production environment; secondly, this system had to have the ability to pass data to and from many other computers and devices without interrupting the design operator. To do this a multi-tasking operating environment was specified and although micro computers had limited capabilities in this field (a typical limitation would be a significant reduction in speed during concurrent activities) none could match the speed and power offered by high performance mini computers running under the Unix environment, (bearing in mind that

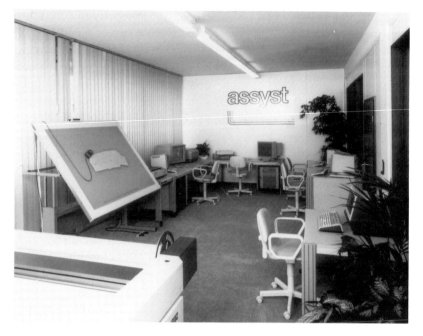

Fig. 3.1. The Assyst CAD system.

Unix is specifically aimed at multi-user/multi-tasking operations). The PDS was a great success and they committed extensive development resources into marker making, grading and automatic pattern generation (discussed in more detail later). This is how the Assyst system came into being (Fig. 3.1).

So now we are back to five systems on the market. There are of course one or two more but the accepted big five are the only ones to have made a significant impact on the world market.

Early marketing directions

In examining the CAD/CAM marketing of the last two decades it is necessary to look at the way in which sales were directed. Who made the first purchases and why?

I came to England in the mid-1970s and opened my own office for marketing CAMSCO systems to the clothing industry. I had only one competitor, the Hughes Apparel System, and I think we both entered the UK market at the same time. The European offices of both companies were already open. The first system in the UK was a CAMSCO sold to Ladybird and they wanted it to drive their Gerber cutter. The second system was sold to a Northern Ireland company making shirts and they bought it to save cloth on the very large orders they received from big retailers. This they achieved by being able to make markers and to know exactly what fabric utilisation they were getting, because the system gave them this information.

As I started to call on customers in the UK I came up against two main problems. The first was the price of a system which started at about £200 000 and meant that this was the most expensive purchase a company had ever made, apart from the building they were housed in (if they owned it). The second problem was that a lot of the customers were supplying the big retail chain groups and were required to submit a sample in each size, say from 8 to 18 for example.

This was not too difficult but when the samples were tried on by the models, in the various sizes, the buyers asked for alterations to be made to the garments. The manufacturer would have to go back to his factory, alter the patterns, remake all the samples and submit them again. In some cases the nested patterns after alterations bore no resemblance to the graded nest he first started out with. A size 12 in one area could be larger than a size 14 etc. I was told on many occasions that if I could get the manufacturer's customer to accept one sample made up and a print out of the nested grade, I would have an immediate system sale.

It was S R Gent who bought the third CAMSCO system in the UK. Their justification was on speed of throughput only; any other benefit would be welcome. It was this company who were the first to submit two samples (12/18) and a nested grade and have it passed for fit. To us, selling systems, this was a great breakthrough. It also had another spin-off. The large retail groups were now telling their suppliers that they should get into this new technology as it would ensure better fit and more accurate patterns. This was wonderful news to us on the marketing side.

Now Gerber took over the Hughes AM1 system and from this they developed the Gerber AM5. It had better software than that of the AM1, the hardware was improved – particularly the screen, and it still used a Hewlett Packard mini computer. By this time they had developed the flat-bed plotters which were not only faster but also did not use the expensive sprocket-fed paper required by the drum plotter.

This was an interesting time from a marketing point of view. A large textile Group made the decision to go into marking and grading systems in a big way. Both Gerber and CAMSCO were asked to quote. We both went in with quotes of about £120 000 per system and we were told that we had to do better than that as the initial order was for about eight systems with more to come. I don't know exactly what went on in the Gerber camp but within CAMSCO UK and CAMSCO Inc. there was great excitement. We were going to get this order. It was obviously the same at Gerber. I cannot remember the exact prices that were quoted back and forth but in the end Gerber won at a greatly reduced price which was between £70 000 and £80 000. The next phase was to be at a higher price, but that order put Gerber fairly and squarely on the UK map. They were also beginning to sell their numerically controlled (NC) cutting systems in the UK – a market which had proved to be the biggest outside the USA.

The Gerber cutter was a boon for the manufacturers who had large capital budgets. Gerber also had worldwide patents on their cutters so they had this segment of the market to themselves. CAMSCO could also drive the Gerber cutter and later all the other makers of CAD/CAM systems could also drive cutters. The marking

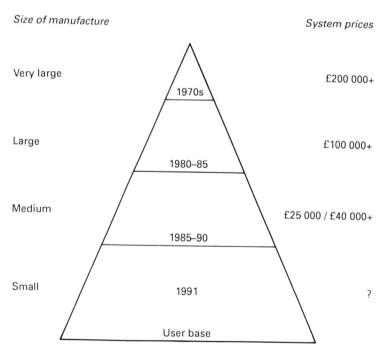

Fig. 3.2. The price pyramid of CAD/CAM systems. The systems sold in the 1970s and early 1980s are now being replaced; as the price of systems comes down so the user base increases.

and grading system was now within reach of a far larger section of the market. The £100 000 barrier had been broken and not long afterwards the £75 000 barrier was also broken. Figure 3.2 illustrates the price pyramid.

The five main CAD/CAM systems

Gerber, who currently operate under the banner of Gerber Garment Technology, absorbed CAMSCO, ceased to market the AM1 and AM5 systems and released the PC based Accumark system. Lectra became well established with their own standard system and cutter. Investronica became well established with a PC based system and they also supply cutters. Microdynamics were in the market place with a PC based system. Assyst arrived here but with a mini computer based system and this is running on the Unix operating system. All other systems are running under MS-DOS/PC-DOS, with the exception of Lectra who wrote their own operating system.

It was with this advent of PC based systems that the market place changed. Prices are as low as £25 000 up to £40 000 for a base system. One of the main reasons for the low price is that hardware prices have come down and the competition in the market place is very fierce.

Grading and marker making

All the systems can grade pattern pieces with various degrees of sophistication and speed. All systems can make markers. Some vendors even claim to have an automatic marker making package but this is little more than a marketing gimmick at the moment because none of the markers produced are efficient enough for a production environment. They often fall short by about 8% to 10% or more. One size costing markers can be achieved with an automatic marking system.

When Assyst selected their hardware from Hewlett Packard, this company had just launched its HP9000/300 Series which had been voted by the engineering world of aerospace, automotive and ship building as the most powerful tool available. This was vindicated by sales of such equipment to the likes of the aerospace industry, Rockwell International, General Motors and many more. It was able to offer connectability to other systems, which meant a buyer of systems could choose different types of system to best suit various applications and have them able to pass information back and forth.

The Assyst PDS package was sold to users of existing systems, again mostly CAMSCO, who connected the PDS workstation to their existing system and passed over block patterns to Assyst's workstation for style creation and grading. Once this was done the graded pieces went back to the existing system, and the markers were made.

Pattern design systems

PDS is widespread in Germany and Italy. In the UK the market was very slow to accept it, with a few notable exceptions, for examples S R Gent and Frank Usher; the former uses Investronica, the latter Assyst. Other companies in the UK used PDS for alterations, e.g. trouser lengths or skirt lengths, but not for the total creation of a style from a basic block, except when the style was very simple. I think this was due to the fact that a lot of our UK production was for the large chain groups who buy fewer styles but in large quantities. In Europe you had small orders, larger style choice and more detail in the garments, which means you had to have fast throughput. I predicted that this would change in the next few years, and it did!

The other new development in the market place of system software is PGS, or pattern generation software. At present the two packages I have seen are from Assyst, called Conex, and from Investronica, called PGS. The following description is a broad overview.

The system has a size table, an alteration table and style listing. There are also up to a hundred questions to answer about various parts of the garment you are making, e.g. the lapel – what width if different from the style you have chosen etc. The system can then create a full set of patterns in all the sizes you have chosen, for the outer fabric, linings and interlinings. Typically 40 sizes can be created in 10 to 20 minutes; this is all the pattern pieces graded (outer, linings and interlinings). This is then transferred to the CAD system from a PC and stored with a style name, piece name and sizes already graded ready for marker making. The market however generally rejected such systems. This was probably due to the demand for fast style.

Computer integrated manufacturing

The popular phrase in computing at the moment is 'Open Systems'. An example of this is the direct transfer of production data to the commercial electronic data processing system for further processing. Any data from any individual system within the factory can be made available to any other computer. This concept is gaining popularity but there is still a long way to go. To implement CIM requires time, money and a lot of nerve. In a lighter context it could be referred to as 'confusion in management'.

THE FUTURE OF COMPUTER AIDED DESIGN SYSTEMS

TIM STEER

Information management

The computer systems used for CAD/CAM must have a high performance and generally offer high speed networking capabilities. This situation has spanned a new area of technology, the function of information management (I.M.).

Integrated CAD/CAM systems hold much of the information which is required as input for paper-based forms or data sheets within a manufacturing environment. Consequently, many CAD/CAM suppliers now offer such an information management package. In principle the CAD/CAM system is networked with all other computers in the company, thereby providing an on-line connection to existing real-time information.

Within an I.M. system, form layouts are made available on a high definition monitor and the user controls how these forms are populated with data. For example, a garment specification sheet may require a bill of materials from the commercial system, a fabric requirement from the CAD/CAM package and a sketch of the garment from the design room CAD system. In addition, the form may also hold a calculation to total the price values from the bill of materials and fabric requirement to provide a total cost of components for a garment. The resulting form can usually be printed on a monochrome or colour laser printer.

With this facility in place it is easy to see how all management information can be manipulated and viewed.

Artificial intelligence

It is not expected that the principal methods of design through cutting will change in the near future. We will continue to design, grade, plan cutting orders, plan lays and optimize numerically controlled cutting etc. However, the way in which these and similar processes are run is likely to change drastically. The reason for such a change will be the introduction of artificial intelligence and expert knowledge bases. For those who are not familiar with these terms, artificial intelligence is a series of software procedures which allow a computer to think in similar ways to that of a human, and an expert knowledge base is a list of procedures which a computer remembers having watched a human 'expert' execute a function, whilst having the ability to offer these functions to a program environment. If you put the two items together you have a very powerful mechanism for learning and assimilating.

Using the technological horizons we can currently view in apparel manufacturing, artificially intelligent computers will balance an entire system from the input of accepted patterns, quantities and restraints to the output of high quality cut parts which will be bundled into the hands of the sewing machine operators. This is the natural interpolation of present and experimental computer system functionality.

Looking deeper, if we consider the grading function we will then see how a very similar procedure could be applied to lay planning, cut order planning and NC cut path sequencing. A grader has an infinite number of possible movements to apply to a given grading point. However, through experience, he/she can reduce this, normally to within a matter of millimetres. Without any prior knowledge a computer would probably make wild guesses as to how a given point would move, very much like a child learning how to draw. However, having watched a human and stored in its expert knowledge base a particular movement on the same type of piece perhaps ten to fifteen times the computer would have the ability to reapply the information with a great deal more accuracy. In this way, and over a period of time, the wild guesses would be more and more accurate. The interesting and almost unbelievable part, however, is that the latest artificial intelligence methods now allow for the computer to offer, after training, a *more* accurate and *faster* solution than a human. Recent advances in artificial intelligence using a technique referred to as neural networking have reached such a peak that a computer can learn to talk in English overnight, learn to walk (using robotics) within minutes, learned, to recognize happy or sad faces and more. Each of these systems have learned using exactly the same processes as a baby's mental activity whilst learning.

This kind of simulation can also be applied to lay planning, bringing success where current mathematical methods of automatic lay planning fall down. Mathematical algorithms cannot push patterns into the selve edge, cannot cut piping in half, cannot overlap pieces where a large seam allowance is obvious, etc. Artificially learned procedures *can* offer these possibilities and more.

Clearly, artificial intelligence is about to become the largest area of impact. It is now within reach for two reasons. Firstly, there was a massive breakthrough in artificial intelligence techniques two to three years prior to this article, which brings the subject into the scope of any serious software graduate (and out of the realms of the silicon valley ivory towers). Secondly, the techniques still require a great deal of performance from a computer and such power is only recently within the budget of many manufacturing companies.

3 dimensional design

Another area where experimental success will reap massive benefits is currently being investigated worldwide – the concept of 3 dimensional garment design. In the UK, de Montfort University is currently developing this concept.

The idea is that, using a powerful computer with a large and crisp monitor, a designer can drape scanned fabrics onto a 3 dimensional model on the screen. Using libraries of garments along with related texture and drape libraries any design could be visualized from any angle and in any lighting, thus providing the most accurately represented garment without it being constructed physically. Furthermore, a pattern cutter could then determine where the cutting lines would occur and the computer would break down the 3 dimensional parts into 2 dimensional flat pattern shapes. These would then be fed into a pattern design package for annotation, engineering and general refining.

Now, imagine the concept of the aforementioned artificial intelligence techniques being applied to a finished and functional 3 dimensional to 2 dimensional pattern creator. This will probably be the dream of the twenty-first century. What has to be clearly stated is that, for both artificial intelligence and 3 dimensional design, human intervention will still, very definitely, be required. The difference between garments is due to humans and this variety will always be important. In addition, UK manufacturing companies must dig deep into their pockets to buy into new technologies and fund the future research.

THE CONSULTANT

Chapter 4
Consultancy in CAD for Clothing and Textiles

PHIL WIGHT

Phil Wight obtained his degree in Electrical and Electronic Engineering at the City University, London. He started his career as an Electronic Engineer and became involved with the clothing industry when he joined Courtaulds, developing computer controlled knitting machines. This was his introduction to the world of computers and he joined CAMSCO when they opened their UK offices in the mid-1970s. He installed the first CAMSCO systems in the UK and became Technical Director of the UK company. On the take-over of CAMSCO by Gerber, he remained as Technical Director of a new company CCS, who became agents for the Investronica System.

In 1986 he formed his own company, Productive Management Systems, to develop software packages for the clothing industry. He took a short break to set up and run the UK branch of Investronica. Once this was established he returned to PMS as a consultant to companies purchasing CAD/CAM technology. He is presently consultant with some of the main clothing manufacturers in the UK.

The need for a consultant

The role of the consultant in the field of CAD/CAM technology has only recently become apparent and necessary to the garment manufacturer. In the past CAD/CAM technology was restricted to grading and marking systems and was available from a limited number of suppliers. The basic CAD system offered three main functions:

(1) *Pattern input* – the digitising of card patterns into a computer system.

(2) *Grading* – the creation of X,Y co-ordinates to generate additional sizes.
(3) *Marking* – the creation of a lay plan via a graphic workstation.

The choice of system was restricted to two main overseas suppliers. With the introduction of the micro-based computer in the early 1980s came the opportunity for other companies to emerge as suppliers of CAD systems. This led to over five additional suppliers offering CAD technology to the garment industry. Of course with the increase in suppliers came competition and the great price war.

At the end of the 1970s a basic CAD system with one display, digitiser and plotter, cost over £100 000. At the end of the 1980s the cost of the same basic system had fallen dramatically to around £40 000.

Competition led to cheaper systems for the garment manufacturer but caused the system supplier to develop less expensive hardware in order to reduce their system selling price.

At the end of the 1980s this price war reached a trough and it became impossible to continue the downward trend in system price. However, the competitive spirit still remained and the system suppliers had to look elsewhere to gain the edge. This has led to the software war and the suppliers are now making available all sorts of software packages to entice the customer to buy their system.

We now have 'buzzwords' floating around the industry, such as CIM (computer integrated manufacturing) and PGS (pattern generation systems). The concept of a CAD system utilised only for grading and marker making is replaced with the CAD/CAM concept of a common database with a totally integrated manufacturing philosophy linking manufacturers' mainframe computers to control production units, resulting in real time data capture of work in progress. And if this is not transparently clear to the reader it could be that the appointment of a consultant is overdue.

What can the consultant offer?

With the introduction of more comprehensive software packages, the decision on the purchase of a CAD/CAM system is no longer based mainly on the price. The potential buyer now has to consider all the new facilities and programs and to evaluate the effectiveness of them as an essential part of the continued viability of his business.

The present trend of introducing a totally integrated manufacturing concept (CIM) using a CAD/CAM system from garment design through pattern development, production and finally dispatch, can leave a potential user completely bemused as to how he can maximise his profitability by the use of a particular CAD/CAM system.

Whether a totally integrated CAD/CAM system can practically be achieved within a garment manufacturer's company at the present time can be comprehensibly debated. A better philosophy to follow would be a step by step method, whereby the introduction of CAD/CAM technology within a company is done over a period of time, being introduced in key areas on a co-ordinated and tightly structured basis, beginning with grading/marking, then design and order processing, and finally manufacturing.

Grading and marker making departments have long accepted CAD/CAM technology as standard. Apart from a few advances in these fields – the most noticeable being automatic marker generation for costing markers (not sufficiently advanced for automatic production markers) – there have been no major developments in these areas.

Most large garment manufacturers have some form of CAD/CAM grading and marking system in use. However, computerised cutting has evolved rapidly since the market was opened for other suppliers to sell these cutters. There is no longer a monopoly in cutters, and as with CAD systems the competition has brought prices down. More companies are looking at introducing this technology.

However, the introduction of computerised cutting into the normal cutting room requires a great deal more consideration and control than may at first sight seem necessary. This is where a consultant can be of most benefit as it is where really significant savings can be achieved. Most cutting room staff do not have any CAD/CAM experience and a major retraining program is required. Obtaining the optimum link between the CAD department and the cutting room is vital for problem-free transfer of data between these operations. A high degree of co-ordinated control is required to avoid incorrect cutting of styles which results in high re-cut cost and fabric wastage.

The consultant can play a vital role in three major areas:

Pre-installation

The consultant will look at the customer's present working methods and in particular at the area where CAD/CAM would be beneficial. Beginning in the design department he will consider the use of concept design systems, and the method of producing new designs and offering these for approval, to customers. Is there a need for a 'sketching system', where first concept design can be created on a graphics display and different fabrics/colours overlaid on to the original sketch to produce a hard copy print out of a new garment design? Will customers accept these designs rather than the traditional sample garments? Or could this be a half-way measure to reduce the number of sample garments?

Presently there are few companies using these sketching systems as an effective replacement for actual garment selection, mainly because present technology has not evolved within the customer selection departments to accept 'designs by floppy'. The main reason is that it is difficult for the selector to obtain a 'feel' for a garment when it is only represented on paper. The cost of these systems is very high at present and the quality of print that can be achieved is not of an acceptable level. However, there are increasing signs that this technology is gradually being accepted by customers and we will certainly see an increase in the number of garment manufacturers buying these sketching systems in the future.

Next comes pattern creation. Most companies still create their hard card patterns by manual methods because present pattern technicians have been trained manually with card patterns and the technology has only recently been available to achieve pattern creation by computer. With the pattern design system (PDS) and more recently pattern generation system (PGS) now available on most CAD/CAM systems, the computerised skills of the manual pattern technician can be utilised more effectively and accurately. These facilities can be used to replace all present methods of manual pattern creation. The benefits of using a CAD system for pattern creation will result in more consistent and accurate patterns, as well as faster responses to design changes.

There is, however, a reluctance by the pattern technicians who have been trained in the traditional ways, to accept this philosophy. This creates a hurdle that requires a great deal of 'educating' or high pressure selling. The good news is that more and more colleges of further education have now gone down this path of computerised pattern creation, and the present pattern technicians entering the industry are trained or at least experienced in the field of computerised pattern design systems.

System survey

A consultant will evaluate present systems on the market and their suitability to the customer's requirements. With at least six major suppliers of CAD/CAM systems now, this is essential. All systems will provide adequate grading and marking functions, but their suitability to fit in with the present methods of grading and marking departments and future development, must be considered. The grading method of the system, the size ranges available and the present identification protocol used on pieces and markers, must be looked at. Is there any link to mainframe computers and production control systems? What additional software features are available that will improve the overall performance of the company?

For a small company interested in grading and marking only the choice of system could be heavily influenced by price, as all grading and marking systems are fairly compatible. The consultant will evaluate each system by visiting the supplier with his client for an initial preview of the system. From these visits he will select two or three systems for a more detailed investigation. Based on the set of parameters drawn up during pre-installation, final selection begins. Certain styles may be selected for trials and these will be carried out on each system selected. The support and back-up services of each supplier will also be taken into consideration.

With advances in computer technology, the choice of hardware used by the supplier will certainly have to be taken into consideration. It is vital that the hardware is up to date and that as far as possible the supplier will not be changing hardware within a short period, leaving the customer with an outdated machine soon after it is installed.

It is not only a matter of deciding which system to purchase, but of how the system be fully utilised to improve the overall performance of the CAD/CAM departments.

Post-installation

The consultant oversees the successful integration of the selected system within the company's organisation, including the implementation of new working procedures to optimise the performance of CAD/CAM technology.

Any main CAD/CAM supplier will be at your beck and call before a decision on the purchase of a system. Once a system has been installed and the initial training period has expired, so does the support and advice from some suppliers. This, however, is the most crucial phase of the introduction of a CAD system. Training may have been carried out on how to use the system in terms of inputting patterns and marker making, but the operation and integration of these procedures within the company becomes a stumbling block. New paperwork to control the flow of work from department to department needs to be created. Other departments connected with the CAD system need to be educated as to what can be achieved from a computerised system, and how they can obtain the best use of this technology.

The introduction of a CAD/CAM system within a company is far more extensive than most companies realise. Generally most CAD/CAM systems are only being utilised to about 60% of their true potential, and in some cases less.

It is after system installation that the failure or success of the project will be decided. All CAD/CAM systems work, but many take much longer to reach the 60% efficiency than is necessary. The use of a consultant can not only achieve this target more speedily and effectively, but can also increase this to 70% or 80%.

The creation of the proper paperwork, not of any fixed format but that which is best suited to the existing methods of workflow in the company, forms the building blocks of a better controlled and managed system. Standard checks can be introduced to avoid costly errors.

The consultant acts as a guiding hand to lead the operators down the shortest and most efficient paths. He is not there to run the system and act as system manager, which is often assumed. He is the adviser to the staff in the appropriate departments, who are the people that must do the work.

The consultant can be important to the garment manufacturer about to embark on the challenging journey of purchasing a CAD/CAM system. Regardless of which system is selected, proper guidance in its implementation within the organisation can be very beneficial to the company. The worry of successfully installing a CAD/CAM system can be transferred to the consultant, leaving the director responsible to embark on yet another journey with only the occasional glance back to see how progress is coming on.

The consultant, as the temporary navigator of the ship, can now guide the crew successfully to their destination in the shortest possible time and with the minimum 'walking the plank' situations. The question for the consultant is what flag will he have flying on the main mast? Will it be French, Spanish, German or American? Could it even be British?

Can the consultant be truly independent?

When deciding which system to recommend to his client, the consultant may be coming on board with a certain flag already in his pocket.

An evaluation of any commodities involves a thorough investigation of the pros and cons. As a result of the findings, a decision is made on which comes out best. It can be assumed that further investigations will always result in one item being selected as the best, and therefore earmarked as the item to recommend.

Although the evaluation may have been based on a set of standard specifications, any investigation must include the suitability of that product to different individuals' needs. A certain product may be best according to the standard criteria, but when individual requirements are taken into account another may be more suitable.

Technology is continually advancing and the system suppliers are striving to maintain this trend. The product of yesterday is seldom the same as today's or tomorrow's. So it is with CAD/CAM systems. Because of the complexity of these systems and the different packages available, it is not possible to evaluate a system purely on set parameters. Parameters have to be devised to evaluate the CAD/CAM system for the particular client. This is achieved during the preinstallation consultancy period. Then during the system selection period the consultant evaluates the present systems on the market and compares them to these parameters.

So the consultant always comes on board with at least five flags in his pocket, and as the journey begins he one by one tosses the flags overboard until there is only one left. This flag he proudly hoists on to the main mast, and yet another and even more challenging journey begins.

The future of CAD/CAM in the clothing industry is an exciting prospect. CAD has remained dormant for too long. The time is ripe for real advances in this technology. New operating systems, networking the processing power of computers together, will lead to more complex systems, and the philosophy of a totally computer integrated management system may at last be on its way.

THE CAD BUREAU

Chapter 5
Making the Grade

TONY WALSH

Tony Walsh graduated from the University of Newcastle upon Tyne in Mechanical Engineering. He later studied at Hollings College, Manchester, gaining a post graduate Diploma in Clothing Management and Technology. He worked for Hepworth Tailoring from 1972, becoming responsible for the installation and management of one of the first CAD systems in the UK clothing industry in 1975. He was involved in the development of this system for made to measure. He helped to set up and run Com Plan Technology Limited as a CAD Bureau for the clothing industry, becoming Managing Director in 1985.

The CAD bureau for the clothing industry

Back in the early days of 1981 when Com Plan Technology was established and CAD bureaux were in their infancy in the UK clothing industry, customers were easily impressed by the technology. For many it was their first real exposure to the use of computers for grading and lay planning and they viewed it with a mixture of awe and fear. If we were to keep those customers we quickly had to lower their expectations of what the technology could offer them and allay their fears by showing them that the CAD system was only a tool – in the hands of an experienced clothing technician a very powerful tool, but useless without the skills of the designer, the grader and the lay planner. The mystique of the 'black box' had to be removed, together with the idea that you pushed a button and it all happened.

Nowhere was this more relevant than in lay planning, where many believed that simply because computers were being used material must be saved. Today our customers are more sophisticated and less easily impressed. For some, coming to a bureau is the first step on the road to having their own in-house CAD system, and the independent bureau can show them if and how CAD can help them and the true cost.

For most, their interest is in the end product and it matters little to them whether we use 'light pen' or 'ink pen' to achieve it. The bureau's primary concern must also be with the end product, and it must use the equipment, and above all the staff, that will enable it to achieve a standard of quality higher than the customer would reach themselves. For what would be acceptable from an in-house source becomes unacceptable when 'we are paying good money for it'. In this respect the bureau is the most severe test of the CAD system and the ability of the staff to run it. It must achieve a consistently high standard, be able to work on ladies fashions, wetsuits, bras and cass-ocks all at the same time, deliver to the clothing industry standard (i.e. yesterday) and, at least as far as the independent bureau is concerned, make a profit.

Design

Design can often be the first stage in the process, but first the term must be defined. The designer can be the person who produces the style sketches or creates the first pattern, and occasionally is both. I like to differentiate between the two functions by calling the first styling and the second pattern design. Styling has no place in our bureau since we believe it would compromise our position. By this I mean that we work on styles from a wide spectrum of eminent customers, and even though it would never be our intention to copy we could not fail to be influenced by what we had seen. Therefore to avoid the suggestion of plagiarism and maintain our professional integrity, we limit our services to pattern design.

I do, however, hold a strong opinion on the relevance of CAD to styling. CAD styling systems are neatly defined by the generic term 'sketch pad' systems, though companies selling these systems prefer to use more elaborate language. It is generally supposed that these sophisticated drawing and colouring machines will stimulate the creativity of the stylists and enable them to produce more styles more quickly. Perhaps this is so, but a competent stylist can visualise a style and efficiently transfer it to paper without the need for this tech-nology, and maybe this is another example of computers being used because they can be rather than because they need to be.

There is a principle of computer applications here that is relevant throughout CAD, and that is that the more a piece of data is used, the cheaper it becomes. The problem with sketch pad systems is that the sketch is the only end product. These systems operate independently, are not linked to the main CAD system and cannot transfer data to it. Work is being done on software that will convert a three-dimensional style concept into a two-dimensional pattern, but a practical solution is a long way off and then we would be asking stylists to produce engineered drawings rather than sketches. CAD systems could be used as a sales tool to show the buyer that there are other options, but all this adds further weight to my argument that sketch pad systems have no place in a production orientated CAD bureau.

Pattern creation

The style concept comes from the customer, usually in the form of a sketch, and it is the bureau's job to translate that into a working first pattern. This is done by referring to our own library of tried and tested basic blocks, but often we find that we have to draft a block from scratch. Our pattern design software is one of the most advanced available, but still we find that while a new pattern can be constructed on a blank screen, it is quicker to draft by hand and then input it to the computer. Under some circumstances this could be different, for example with a large product range over a narrow band of product types, and a design technician totally dedicated to the application of CAD to pattern construction, i.e. he or she is doing it all day, every day. In essence, CAD pattern construction is a 'use or lose' type of skill and therefore only finds a place in the largest design rooms, where its potential for standard pattern manipulations done quickly and accurately can be fully exploited. Strangely it is often this aspect of CAD software that (after price) is used to determine which system is purchased, and for most it will be the software which is least used.

When a block pattern has been established on the computer system the situation is very different, for the basic structure can be manipulated, dissected and reconstituted to create the desired styles, with the speed and accuracy expected of computers. We do this extensively in our bureau and will do so even more as we learn new applications for this aspect of CAD. The principle of block design is vital to the successful application of CAD in pattern design, meaning that many styles can be created from few blocks. The stylists must be encouraged to view their styles in this way, while not compromising their creative freedom. The fact that the bureau will charge less for pattern design from an existing block than creating a new block introduces a discipline that will help to concentrate the mind of the stylist.

Grading

The next stage in the bureau process is grading. Contrary to popular belief this can be a slow and painful process in CAD because time and skill are required to establish the grading data on the system. The computer grader must input the pattern to the computer, interpret the size chart, build the rules on the computer, apply those rules, and plot out and check the grade. The manual grader will move and mark the pattern to the size chart, checking as he goes.

It is when the grading data is established that the speed of computers can be exploited, by reusing the grading rules on similar styles. However, it is not an automatic process and can never be taken for granted. Good grading skills are needed to check the output from the CAD system and to manipulate the data to achieve perfection. After grading we invariably submit a full size nest to our customer for approval because, while the grade is technically correct, there will be other ways of doing it and the customer must agree with the method used. If grading using CAD is to be cost effective it is important that, as far as possible, the grading system is standardised so that grade data can be reused. This will rarely be absolute since even slight changes in line or seam placement may require a change to the grade rules. But now it is more a case of modifying rather than creating grading systems.

Fortunately, in the vast majority of cases, our advice is accepted. Indeed I can recall only one customer who was insistent that each style in his range was unique and should be graded differently. Our advice was that in those circumstances CAD was of no help to him. Our attitude to our customers in this, as in all aspects of our services, is that the customer is always right, even when he is wrong, but we reserve the right to tell him we think he is wrong.

Once a grade has been approved by the customer the style may proceed to pattern production or lay planning and occasionally both. The only additional pieces of information needed for pattern production are the sizes in the grade which are to be produced in card form, and the quality and colour (or colours) of the card required. Most orders are then completed and despatched within 24 hours.

We may also be asked to produce a pattern with different stretch or shrinkage factors from those allowed for in the original pattern. We simply need to know the increase or decrease in the warp and weft allowance and that change can be made automatically and a new pattern produced. The changes will be applied proportionately throughout the whole pattern so that the balance and fit of the original pattern are maintained.

Lay planning

Lay planning is a more complex issue and full details must be known of the cutting situation in which the lay plans are to be used. There are the physical constraints such as the usable cloth width, the table space available and the order ratio; and practical constraints like the cutting equipment and the skill of the cutting staff. A bureau must know and understand all the factors that will influence the cutting of the order, and must produce lay plans that will work in the customer's chosen cutting room. All lay planning, whether CAD based or manual, is a compromise between the efficiency of the lay (i.e. how tight it is) and how easy it is to cut. The art of lay planning is in balancing these two conflicting interests.

There is a popular misconception among those who have not used CAD, or at least not for production lay planning, that the lay planning process in CAD is automatic, meaning that you press a button and the computer unassisted produces the perfect lay plan. The truth is somewhat different. Lay planning is essentially a creative process requiring good spacial awareness, and not everyone has the ability to do it. It is not a jigsaw puzzle with a perfect solution in which each piece has only one possible position; it is a compromise between material and cutting efficiencies in which each piece has an infinite number of possible positions and orientations. Computers are particularly inept at dealing with processes in which there is a creative element, and the trial and error approach is limited by the possible variations. Sophisticated algorithmic programs have now been developed by most system manufacturers to approximate the skill of the human lay planner, and that is just what they do with predictable results.

Automatic lay planning will produce lays requiring 2% to 5% more fabric, with poor cutting characteristics. But progress is being made in this area of development and no one can predict how quickly the technology will take us there. When it does I will be the first in line to buy, for I would love to be able to guarantee to every customer that I can save them material. Of course automatics can be used for rough costings, where all that is required is an approximation of the material usage, but customers are not interested in approximations.

So for now and the foreseeable future our only option is interactive marker making, i.e. using man and machine. The only difference between what we are doing and what our customers are doing is that we have skilled lay planners sat in comfortable chairs moving patterns around electronically, while they have skilled lay planners running around tables with pieces of cardboard. A lay planning service gives customers time, for a CAD system enables lay plans to be produced quickly at a consistently high level of material utilisation. How much material is saved depends on how good or bad the customer's lay planners are and how long he is prepared to let them work on each lay plan.

Where orders are small, garments are simple and fabric is cheap, CAD lay planning is a total overkill and not cost effective. Bureaux must be the first to recognise this and advise customers accordingly.

The end product of lay planning is usually marker making, i.e. producing full size copies of the lay plans. Where a customer has in-house diozo type copying facilities all we need to supply is one master copy of each marker. For the remainder, copies can be ordered as and when required and are normally despatched within 24 hours.

For customers who are factoring the product through cut, make and trim in the UK or abroad, a costing marker is required; therefore only a material rating figure, possibly with a miniature copy marker, is needed. Armed with the bureau's engineered production patterns and accurate material usage figure, the customer can negotiate a realistic price with his supplier. Also, because the customer owns the data he has paid to have developed, he can quickly source the product elsewhere should problems arise, or can have a parallel supplier with the confidence that at least in terms of fit and fabric cost the product will be the same.

Confidentiality and data ownership

Title to the data put and stored on bureau computer systems lies with the customer who paid for it to be put there. Data cannot be transferred to, or used for, the benefit of a third party without the specific written instructions of the first party – the customer. This has occasionally meant refusing data on styles to very large companies and organisations who we know own those styles, but they were brought to us for processing by the supplier and it is the supplier who pays us to create the data. Invariably this problem is resolved by the supplier transferring the data to his customer, but the principle is inviolable.

Apart from the ownership of the data, security is also very important. To those companies who invest heavily in the development of patterns, those fragile pieces of card can represent the life blood of the company. When fire, flood or some other disaster has struck one of our customers, we have been able to replace patterns within hours or days.

Servicing the customer

The essence of a successful CAD bureau in the clothing industry is service. As an independent bureau unencumbered by association with, or ownership by, any system supplier, college, local authority or garment manufacturer, we are able to dedicate ourselves to the service of our customers. Maintaining a reputation for quality and service, in our case, takes over 20 staff, almost all of whom are highly skilled clothing technicians, designers, graders or lay planners, they operate a shift system to ensure that services are available to customers from 7am to 9pm on week days throughout the year, closing only for bank holidays.

The CAD system enables us to fully utilise our skills for the benefit of the customers. We recruit and train skilled clothing technicians, not computer operators. CAD operation can be learned quickly, but the skills of the clothing technician can take a lifetime to master.

The CAD bureau's customers are anybody involved with patterns. I am constantly surprised and gratified by the range of products and size of companies that come to us: the one-person design consultant who will use our services to enhance his or her own; the small design companies with two or three people who are factoring their production and need technical support in pattern design, sizing and grading and material costings; the small manufacturers, where our services will release the designer (or owner) to do what he or she wants to do, i.e. design; the medium size companies who can no longer find or afford the in-house skills, yet must maintain and improve quality of fit and the efficiency of material usage; the large multi-site company where consistency and control are essential; and the CAD user who needs support in times of machine or people breakdown, or help over seasonal peaks.

For all these customers the first questions are: how much and when – in that order. Companies that do not have in-house resources against which to compare bureau charges can find that the prices for this professional service are little more than they would pay their plumber and a lot less than they would pay their accountant. Where comparisons can be made the company only has to consider that a bureau does not require sick or holiday pay and is only there when needed, to conclude that the services can be cost effective.

As to 'when', the conversation goes something like this:

Bureau   'When do you want it?'
Customer 'Yesterday will do, but the day before would be better.'
Bureau   'When do you need it?'
Customer 'Tomorrow.'
Bureau   'When does it go into production?'
Customer 'Next month.'
Bureau   'OK, let's agree a schedule.'

And so we agree a delivery schedule, and in a properly scheduled production plan there is no waiting time. But despite fax machines, modem links and overnight delivery services, it has to be admitted that the bureau cannot react as fast as the in-house CAD system, and it is logistics more than cost that will encourage the larger customers to buy their own CAD system. It is not the bureau's job to promote CAD, *per se*; indeed, because we have to fulfil the promises we make, we show CAD 'warts and all', but that is inevitable if we are playing our proper role. Hence it is more with pride than regret that we see customers installing and using their own equipment, having evaluated their needs and set their standards by the services we provided.

The future of the CAD bureau

Judging by our own recent investments in buildings and equipment, the CAD bureau faces an optimistic future. While CAD systems are much cheaper than they used to be and in real terms, at least, will continue to fall in price, buying a piece of equipment is not the whole story. I would guess that at least 80% of those who buy systems find they need to increase their budgets after the first year by 30% for capital, and 50% for labour and other revenue items. Companies who need to control their expenditure will continue to look to bureaux to provide CAD services at a budgeted cost.

CAD system manufacturers are now providing programs that will allow their systems to interface with competitors' equipment, thus enabling data transfer between different systems. Therefore I see the bureau playing an increasing role in supporting CAD users. But the most important factor is the continuing decline of sound technical skills in the industry. The bureau will deliver those professional skills using the latest CAD technology and based on a deep understanding of customer needs and the meaning of the word service.

THE USERS

Chapter 6
The Impact of Computer Graphics on Clothing Design

CLIVE WALTER

After graduating from Brunel University, Clive Walter worked in the defence and electronic industries. He joined Marks and Spencer twenty-five years ago, where he has specialised in manufacturing technologies which improve the effectiveness of the company's supply base. He is a Chartered Engineer, and a Fellow of the Institution of Mechanical Engineers, the Institution of Electrical Engineers and the Institute of Quality Assurance.

Customer requirements

What is it that attracts a customer to a garment in a store? The initial impact will be its colour and the design on the fabric, be it the stripe on a shirt, the print on a blouse, the lace on a slip or the jacquard on a jumper. These, together with its shape, give an immediate visual impression – an instinctive feeling of like or dislike. There are other factors too, such as how the fabric feels when handled, how well the garment is made, how comfortable it is and how well it will wear. These add up to give a perception of the garment quality. The major purpose of the clothing and textile industry is to provide garments that will sell and give satisfaction to discerning customers.

Use of CAD

CAD, with its ability to simulate these visual impressions, is currently creating much excitement in the industry. Why? How is CAD being used? What changes are occurring? What is the significance of these changes? How will CAD develop? Interesting questions – the answers to which will emerge from consideration of how a garment is developed from the initial design to its planned production.

Before doing so, however, it is worth considering the historical perspective of CAD, which is not new to the industry.

CAD in fabric design

Some of the earliest applications of CAD occurred in fabric production, when mechanical programming by chains and steels was replaced by relays, actuators and other electronically controllable mechanical devices. In knitting and sock machines it is the selection and movement of needles and beds that is programmed, whereas in weaving it is the selection of warp threads. On CAD systems any sequence of selection to produce the required design can be simulated as a grid on a monitor. Each square on the grid is given a colour corresponding to a knitted loop or woven thread. Computers are thus able to give a visual image of the knitted jacquard or a striped or checked fabric. Both colour and sequence are easily changed as the design process is refined. Once complete, the electronic information is transferred to control the mechanism of the production machines.

CAD in clothing design

The clothing industry has also made good use of CAD. It happened when an alternative to the manual method of using a reciprocating straight knife was developed by Gerber. It was the numerically controlled, plunge knife, automatic cutter. This required the definition of the digital information which describes the shape of the pattern pieces, together with the sequence in which they should be cut.

Computer technology came to the rescue. The shapes of cardboard pattern pieces are given X and Y co-ordinates by a digitiser and entered into a computer. This enables pattern shapes to be displayed on a monitor. Grading, or how each pattern shape changes to allow for different sizes, is automatically achieved. For this to happen the displacement for each significant point on the pattern edge is determined by a set of 'grade rules'.

Planning how the patterns should be nested together in a lay plan to ensure maximum usage of fabric, has become an interactive routine between an operator and computer screen. All the pattern pieces required for a given cut ratio are displayed in miniature, and these are manipulated, rotated and fitted together between two lines which relate to the fabric width. The finished lay plan forms the basic information required to describe the path of the automatic fabric cutter. This information is passed to the mechanisms which control the path of the cutter and other machine functions.

Pattern modification systems have been developed which enable basic pattern shapes to be altered for different style and construction features. Computer technology is used in the whole of the process from pattern design to the control of the cutting machine.

Historical perspective

The historical perspective, therefore, is that CAD has developed from the production requirement and progressed to the technical aspects of design. In many instances CAD has stayed within the production environment, and in this environment designs are offered which can be produced easily and economically. In principle this is commendable but there is a danger that production considerations may restrict design.

Computer colour graphics

The advent of computer colour graphics has changed this perspective by giving designers an innovative tool which is challenging their expertise. The scope of CAD has been extended to include the whole spectrum from design initiation and decision making through to technical design, with the subsequent link to production plant and machinery.

The garment design process

Garment design, like all design, does not exist in a vacuum; it has to respond to the perceived needs of customers in the marketplace. Necessity is said to be the mother of invention; it is equally true of garment design. An understanding of customer needs is of paramount importance, particularly where garments are sold to a mass market.

The retailer is well placed to define precisely those customer needs. Major retailers nowadays operate worldwide. They have knowledge of selling patterns in stores, and they keep up to date with fashion trends and fabric, yarn and component developments. They also keep aware of what is new and what is being sold in the major capitals of the world. This enables them to forecast and give clear directional guidance to their fabric and garment suppliers on predicted customer needs in the season ahead.

The garment manufacturers' designers also keep abreast of fashion trends, receive the directional guidance, and have a knowledge of the production requirements of their manufacturing plants. From this they can offer designs which they consider satisfy the perceived customer need.

All this sounds very straightforward. In reality, it is an iterative process, particularly in a fast changing fashion scene, with design ideas proposed, discussed and modified. Fabric, colour, fabric design, lace and trimmings, silhouette and cost all need to be determined before a decision to place a contract is made. Even then the iterative process continues as the garment is developed, and the technical aspects of fit, grading, construction and garment performance are considered.

It is said that design is 10% inspiration and 90% perspiration. The perspiration is the iterative nature of design, the exploration of different options in order to achieve a coincidence between the designer's creativity and the customer's perceived need, at an acceptable cost.

To sum up, the design process passes through four stages:

(1) *Design initiation stage*, in which the marketplace customer's perceived needs are defined in terms of colour, silhouette, style and fabric design.
(2) *Design concept stage*, when many design options are explored and result in design offers which satisfy the defined criteria of customer needs.
(3) *Decision making process*, where design offers are considered, ranges are developed and decisions to purchase are made.
(4) *Technical design stage*, where the design offer is refined to precisely satisfy the fit, construction, garment performance and production requirements.

Creating visual images

Computer colour graphic systems provide a powerful tool for both the retailer and the garment designer. They choose and change colour to determine a colour design palette; simulate printed, woven and knitted fabrics; and visualise garment accessories and components such as lace and embroidery. They create an image of garment style by texture mapping fabric simulation on to sketches of silhouettes. Specialised software is used to achieve a realistic 3D look to a 2D image.

Designs can be displayed in several ways:

- Firstly on a high resolution graphics monitor, where initial design concepts can be rapidly, easily and inexpensively altered.
- Secondly, printed on paper, generally for presentation purposes to support theme boards, but also to give a better impression of large images.
- Thirdly, printed on to fabric by a thermal transfer or ink-jet printing route. This sample design fabric is made into garments for design and buying review.

In all these display media the image illustrates the proposed garment colour, fabric design and shape – just the attributes that initially attract a customer when they enter a store.

Significance of computer graphics

The significance and benefits of computer graphics during the design initiation and design concept stages can be considered as:

Better communication

A picture is worth a thousand words. A visual image that bears a close resemblance to the finished product enhances the communication between designers and buyers, between sales and marketing, between buyers and stores and within departments and organisations.

Production innovation

CAD systems provide the designer with powerful tools to be more creative. An example of this is with fabric prints. In this case the garment designer is not constrained to an existing fabric design on a sample length. Co-ordinated looks can be achieved by transforming elements of a design across a garment range. In childrenswear the design can be scaled to a specific garment size. Border prints can be added. More complex prints and graphics are now offered as the fabric print is designed for the garment and not vice versa.

More considered design offer

Both the designer and the buyer are able to explore quickly, inexpensively and thoroughly the design options, be it colour, fabric design or shape. The opportunity for this collaboration occurs with:

- the monitor display
- with prints on paper
- with garments made from sample fabric prints.

It is a process of 'refinement by rejection' with the objective of making a single sample garment 'right first time' which is acceptable and bought.

With more traditional methods the time between the design concept and seeing a garment or fabric sample can be extended, particularly when change is requested. This can lead to a compromise decision when time runs out, with neither the designer nor the buyer completely satisfied with the design offer.

Greater responsiveness

Garment development times are shortened. For example, a colour development palette printed on paper is produced in 2–3 days, its fabric equivalent based on laboratory dyed fabrics used to take in excess of six weeks. Sample ink-jet fabrics are made into garments in under one week, whereas a typical print strike off would not be available in under four weeks.

Decisions on garment offers are being made closer to the launch date.

Changes to the garment range are made within the buying season, once the sales patterns are known. The garment offer is more responsive to the immediate customer needs as the garment offer more truly reflects what is and is not selling.

Reduction in design costs

As designers and buyers gain experience with CAD, the more confident they become in their decision making process, for the following reasons:

- It is less costly to decide on design concepts on a high resolution monitor than printed paper.
- It is less costly to decide a design concept on paper than on an ink-jet sample fabric.
- It is less costly to decide on a design concept on an ink-jet sample than a first printed fabric, woven or knitted sample.

- It also takes considerably less time. All this adds up to a reduction in design costs or a more productive design studio.

Technical challenges

This changing role of design and use of computer graphics is however presenting challenges that need to be resolved.

Remote group working

The electronic communication of pictures of high resolution with true colour representation will be needed at speed and at an affordable cost. Such interactive communication could be needed between the garment designer and the retailer, between the garment designer and the fabric or component designer, and between the garment designer and the production source, in all cases both locally and internationally. Development continues on fast transmission links and data suppression techniques.

Data integration

Connectivity or the transfer of structured design information through-out the whole product design and development chain, is required if the benefits of responsiveness and reduced costs are to be achieved. For example, a fabric print created in a garment design department should be capable of electronic transfer to a fabric printer. Colour separations determined on computer should be capable of transfer to screen production systems such as laser engravers. Colour co-ordinates should be capable of transfer to dye prediction and colour kitchens to achieve the desired colour in production. The information flow should be two-way with each stage communicating the detailed needs of each process in the chain.

It is vital to ensure that the visual images created at the design stage – 'What you see' – are faithfully reproduced in production – 'What you get'.

Colour management

This is the most important technical issue. A consistent true colour regime is desirable, in which the colour seen on different monitors and printers (paper or fabric), responding to the same colour co-ordinates, is the same both within a system and between systems.

Considerable progress has been made recently. There is a commercially successful application in which colours developed on a monitor can be accurately reproduced on both dyed fabrics and printed on paper. This operates in a controlled calibrated environment, the challenge is now to develop it into an open system.

Computer aided design department

The advent of CAD has been an engine of change in the Clothing Design Department. Textile designers now work in these departments in close collaboration with their clothing design colleagues. Together they provide a co-ordinated design response to the retailers' requirements, integrating fabric, garment, packaging and component design. This can extend to visualising how a garment might look in a simulated retail environment.

Additionally designers must be even more aware of garment costs, a design concept must respond to market needs, but also be affordable. Here pattern design, costings and product data management systems are used as the garment is developed through the various stages of the design process. Design departments are a fulcrum of activity, and using more high tech equipment to aid their task.

All this has placed increased demands on management who require the skills necessary not only to motivate creative designers but also to cope with and understand the application of sophisticated computer based equipment. Training needs for designers are increased as they widen their knowledge of textile, clothing component and packaging design, together with the associated production techniques.

How will CAD develop?

The uptake of CAD technology in the clothing industry has been rapid. Clothing companies have been very innovative with their applications. They have successfully used it particularly to improve presentation and communication in the marketing of their products.

Technology developments also continue at a pace. Computers are faster, high resolution digital cameras are becoming available, and data storage and retrieval requirements are being addressed. Information from various media sources, video, photography, sound, and graphics can all be put together into multi-media presentations.

Where next? Two applications are emerging:

(1) More effective archiving of design intelligence, to include the

history from previous seasons, together with image databases of new fabrics, components and fashion trends.

(2) Animation of images to achieve a simulated catwalk or store environment. It is advantageous to be able to visualise how a fashion statement might look at the time when design decisions are made about individual products and ranges.

Of these two, the first is more easy to achieve, the second challenges the current level of technology.

Design and market led production

At the beginning of this chapter the question was asked, 'Why is computer aided design currently creating much excitement in the industry?' The answer is the application of computer graphics within both the marketing and design environments. This is giving effective communication of consumer needs, and a creative, speedy response to those needs.

Designers are encouraged to be more creative and bring fresh ideas to the marketplace to attract customers. The industry is being design and market-led with design challenging production.

Chapter 7
CAD in the 'Real World': Using CAD Clothing/Textile Systems in Industry

ROZ DAVIES

After graduating in Clothing Management from the London College of Fashion, Roz Davies started her career as an Industrial Engineer at Reldan Ltd where she practised fundamental Production Management techniques in clothing manufacture. She moved to the London Design Studio of Slimma Casualwear as a production engineer using her knowledge at the 'front end' of the business in the costing and development of new products.

An extension of this role was pursued when she moved to Courtaulds Leisurewear and carried out special projects in the manufacturing divisions before setting up the position of Technical Manager in the London Design Studio. This position has involved the management and development of computer aided design, product costings, total quality and the sample machine room.

Introduction

The phrase CAD in the 'real world' emphasises the day to day productivity requirements that a CAD tool will have to cope with in an ever demanding industrial environment. There is an excitement and frustration in taking theory into practice and continually improving our processes of design and product development to give us a competitive edge.

As Technical Manager of Courtaulds Leisurewear Design Studio, my role has developed into looking at and introducing new methods of working in the design, product development and manufacturing process. Earlier experience in clothing management and industrial engineering, and later experience in quality and design management, has meant an increasing interest in CAD for the last two and a half years. Only now do I feel that I have a clear understanding of what is required to take the industry positively through the 1990s.

My view will very much reflect the mass production and large retail chain store side of the business, but I believe every supplier in the clothing and textile industry will be looking to achieve excellence in:

- design
- quality
- delivery
- price

Understanding the total CAD offer

Business vision

One of the most important aspects of assessing CAD equipment is getting the business to decide on its overall vision of the future. This vision should not just be general statements of annual turnover and shareholders' return on investment; it should also include strategies on how this is going to be achieved. The clothing industry is too clever at blaming the weather or trends in fashion to avoid the issue of looking into the future rather than just the next few months. We also suffer from our traditional view of the regular three year cycle – good year, mediocre year, bad year, etc. – which we believe will happen whatever plans for change we put into action. We must alter this approach.

The successful consideration of CAD investment will be dependent on the business qualifying its objectives for the future, supporting this with a willingness to change, and specifying financial commitment. These are high demands but I believe that this is the only way of managing a successful long term future.

Once the objectives are in place, there is a structure round which to plan the CAD strategy and take advantage of development and innovation to ensure competitive edge. This technology can revolutionise a business and we must make sure we are on the side that wins!

Who should be looking?

This always seems to be a difficult issue as when computers first came into the industry they were certainly not user friendly to the skilled marker maker, pattern grader or cutting room manager. In the last ten years attitudes and computers have changed enormously, but as users we have become more demanding. Because of this it is important to achieve a project team with a balance of knowledge, expertise and seniority:

Applications expert

Someone who understands all aspects of the design and product development is needed. They must want to change the process and have the ability to sell new ideas and put them into practice. Being controversial and innovative is a distinct advantage. It is this person who should lead the project.

Computer expert

The fast growing development of PC technology, communications and connectivity means that in-house or consultancy support is still needed. As needs become more sophisticated investment in the best tools for each job will be wanted. These might not all come from the same supplier.

Business director

At the end of the day financial support will be needed to put the investment proposal into action. To achieve this a business director must be involved, to understand the opportunities that this type of technology can give the business and champion these views in the boardroom.

For final decision making a broader business involvement will be necessary.

What is available?

To examine what is available, it is essential to know something about the product design activities involved in CAD. These are:

(1) Design
(2) Illustration
(3) Pattern design

(4) Product cost
(5) Sample cutting
(6) Sample making
(7) Product specification
(8) Marker making

It is now possible to apply CAD technology to all these areas apart from sample making, and even that process would be improved if CAD were used in the other areas.

2D Graphic Design

A computer tool with graphic capabilities allows the user to scan in or create on screen many types of images, and then manipulate them with the use of various facilities. The quality, capability and prices vary enormously in this technology. It has proved to be a valuable asset to design, illustration and selection. Issues, important to the industry are cost, colour, high image resolution, greater sensitivity to the designer and links in the supply chain.

Pattern design

A computer tool allows the user to scan, digitise in or create pattern blocks on screen, apply grades and redesign pattern pieces where necessary. There are several of these systems available with similar functions and price ranges. Some of them have embraced the future worldwide reduction in pattern technology skills, and some have not. Ease of use, speed of use and communications will be fundamental issues for the future in this area.

The possibilities of designing and pattern cutting in 3D are not as far away as we think!

Costing systems

A computer tool allows quick and easy access to standard minute, trim and fabric databases for the calculation of a full product cost. As we gradually become more professional in business the need for accurate product costings and the monitoring of cost fluctuations become paramount.

Progress in this area seems to have been slow, which has always been a surprise to me. Maybe the industry does not want to know the truth! Accurate data collection, maintenance, ease of use and interpretation into the design environment are important aspects.

Sample cutting

An automatic cutting tool is driven by a pattern design system with the ability to cut single-ply fabric fast.

The process of cutting and making samples is very expensive. The aim with 2D graphic design is to reduce this, but we must also be aware that growth in product ranges and other developments will also affect sample making. Therefore it must be made more cost effective, with quicker response time and greater accuracy. The capability to cut single ply without paper patterns and without using valuable manpower time and skill, can only be an asset.

Production specification

A computer allows a graphic image to be displayed with a product description and a specification of make-up in one facility. Today some part of the manufacturing facility is normally abroad, which has resulted in the need to bring back the use of production specification. This will be the amalgamation of information already compiled, so it will need to be linked to all the other systems and probably customised for company's own needs.

Marker making

A computer tool enables pattern pieces to be placed on to a fabric lay. This is the area which has seen the greatest CAD application so far and most of us rely on it totally. It might need up-dating to take advantage of its new ease of use, cheaper maintenance, increased speed and connectivity.

Will it really work?

One of the problems of visiting computer shows, CAD/CAM suppliers' showrooms and the like, is the difficulty of telling the good from the bad, the real from the contrived. The best solution is to take your own work, on which you can see demonstrations in real time. An even better solution is to have the system on trial in your own premises, which would mean you could use it as your first stage of the learning curve.

Talking to other users can be useful; they will normally tell you the truth. But never forget that CAD/CAM suppliers are always trying to sell you something. It is very important to look at maintenance agreements, company growth and profitability, and the company's view on future developments.

What are the developments?

A strong approach to developments is an essential requirement for CAD technology. Gauging the time span of computer software and hardware issues is difficult but a logical and well planned programme should provide some protection from this. It is important for users to drive the suppliers' research and development teams in the right direction to ensure practical solutions to problems. We must also share our visions of the future so they can maintain a lead on our progress. I have already mentioned the areas in which I feel existing equipment could be improved, but perhaps more collaboration between CAD suppliers, the clothing and textile industry and education could enhance innovative thought. At present computer integrated manufacture seems to be the name of the game, with gradual development into the retail business and the supply chain.

Encouraging investment in CAD

Proposing CAD investment can be one of the most challenging problems. There are no easy solutions; enthusiasm and dedication are essential, and sometimes aggressive behaviour might be necessary!

The world of product design is often seen as being artistic, emotive, unpredictable and of course uncontrollable. This view can be solely due to historical and traditional behaviour patterns. We must now realise that with the introduction of technology we have to look at this environment in a new light. We need to consider the costs of product design while maintaining an atmosphere of creativity and innovation.

The key issues for encouraging CAD investment are:

(1) *Education* This is two-fold, educating the business about product design and CAD equipment.
(2) *Costs* Establishing true costs of present methods of working, with particular emphasis on lead times.
(3) *Payback* Establishing a new approach to payback calculations involving hard and soft benefits.

Each CAD investment will have its own characteristics but it is normally the hard benefits that are easier to quantify, although the soft benefits are more powerful.

Hard benefits

- *Speed* Offering the customer a change in print design or pattern construction in minutes rather than days.
- *Accuracy* Removing silly human errors from pattern making and using consistent information databases.
- *Productivity* Providing a tool to increase productivity by 100% or 200%.
- *Communication* Systems with communication links for quick response and elimination of repeated work.
- *Information* New easy information like pattern stitching measurements for thread calculation and so on.

Soft benefits

- *Quality design service*
- *Informed sales service*
- *Quality product design*
- *Manufacturing flexibility*

Application of CAD in Courtaulds

One of the advantages of working for a large organisation like Courtaulds Textiles plc is that there is always some involvement at senior management level in the development of new technology applicable to our business. On this occasion the liaison link had been established with Computer Design Inc (CDI), an expert software house in America who were developing at that time 2D and 3D design systems for the apparel industry. It became possible, with the co-operation of CDI and the hardware suppliers, to install this equipment at one of Courtaulds Clothings' larger design studios.

The equipment consisted of:

- 1 Silicon graphic workstation with 2D concept design software.
- 1 PC workstation with 2DPC concept design software.
- 1 Howtech scanner.
- 1 Seiko D-Scan thermal printer.
- Ethernet cable to network the configuration.

Fig. 7.1. Courtaulds studio.

This is a 2D graphic design tool to assist design, sales and marketing and visual communications (Fig. 7.1).

The businesses to benefit from this opportunity were Courtaulds Leisurewear and Childrenswear with their interest in print design as well as garment design. Introducing new techniques and technologies into a creative environment was an ambitious challenge, particularly when there was no one to follow. The first stages were very basic: finding space, operator manpower, technical support from Courtaulds Information Services and myself as project manager. The next stage was training for the operators in America, establishing methods of working, measures of evaluation and acceptance into the business.

Training

We assumed that to operate a computer in the design environment we needed practical people, so we selected two experienced pattern cutters to train as operators. They went on a two week training course during which they were taught all aspects of the software. Once back in the working environment we immediately set to work to produce valuable services to our design departments. To become an expert full-time user the learning curve was around 3 to 4 months.

Fig. 7.2. Courtaulds design work.

Methods of working

To ensure computer work was not lost, disciplines of filing procedures and administration had to be introduced. Once these were established, finding work that had been carried out months before became possible. The next area was setting the colour palettes of the season. Great care was taken to produce good quality colour palettes, which immediately have an effect on the quality of computer graphic design work. If we wanted to show our print designs on real garments, we would also have to organise a professional photographic session. We would make white samples in the correct fabric type and have quality photographs taken so we could ensure the highest standard of computer image (Fig. 7.2).

Measures of evaluation

This was a major contribution on which the success or failure of the trial would be decided. The process was via a questionnaire measuring the:

• Image colour
• Image clarity

- Speed of response
- Accuracy to designer's brief
- Clarity of design brief

There was also an area for general comments. It was here that we began to pick up comments like 'I would not have attempted this without CAD', or 'I could not have done this without CAD'.

The evaluation took place over three months so we had plenty of details from which to analyse the appropriateness of CAD to our business. The result was positive and we wanted the equipment as an on-going facility in our design studio. The financial issue was a lot harder to illustrate and I must thank the business leaders for supporting the gamble with this 'leading-edge' technology. I would like to point out that many of our competitors have followed our lead.

Acceptance by the business

As the installation was initiated by a trial it took some time for the business to accept that the technology belonged to them. It took many talks, demonstrations and presentations to educate ourselves, and of course our customers, about the benefits of having such a tool. This education process is continual as new people become involved in the business.

Two and a half years on

The design and sales function could not 'survive' without it. Our method of working has evolved and I believe we are the only 2D graphic design users that have around 15 designers capable of using the technology, and we are training more every day. With designer users we have discovered new requirements for the system and a sensitive bit-pad and pen with many types of drawing tools is becoming a fundamental need. Quality of output is also a big issue and once we have sorted these areas out the scope will be almost unrestricted.

It has been exciting to see the general acceptance of the facility, which is used to illustrate about 60% of our prints and most of our sketch presentation boards. The interest in using it as a designers' tool has varied from 'really keen' to 'if I have to', the latter being a minority of about one out of twenty.

I now feel quite happy about introducing any new technology into the design studio because they all have an understanding of the trials and tribulations you get at the beginning, and the reward of getting the tool to do the job for you and improve your own way of working.

Improvement has been made in communications across the supply-chain with support from technology links.

Courtaulds support of CAD continues with investments at St. Pancras Way in:

- Concept II Ormus Fashion – for creative CAD graphics
- GGT Accumark – for concept pattern design
- Canon Laser Copier 300 – a must for any design studio.

A competitive future with CAD

We have to analyse the business we are in and identify possible solutions, in order to achieve excellence in:

- design
- quality
- delivery
- price

Our final customer is now becoming more informed, more sophisticated and more aware of his/her purchasing power and selection. We have to ensure we provide that 'value added' product that they will choose above others. In addition to the requirements above, we will need to offer quick response.

Quick response

We have now reached the time when we as clothing manufacturers have to respond directly to the behaviour of our final customer and use this as information to help drive our business forward. To do this we must use technology in our processes and in our links to the other processes in the supply chain (Fig. 7.3).

This approach is already being keenly pursued by European and North American clothing manufacturers and we are in a position where we need to catch up. Setting up teams of experts across the supply-chain processes, so we can develop common goals and objectives with logical and practical investment proposals and installations, will lead to a successful future.

It will be the 'best users of CAD' supporting a 'value added'

So the future could look like this:

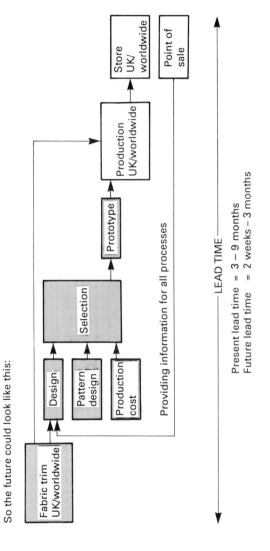

Fig. 7.3. Use of CAD in the supply chain.

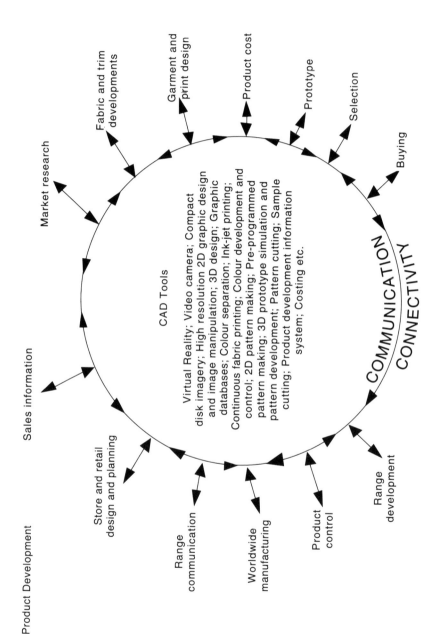

Fig. 7.4. CAD and Product Development. Each business can develop as it sees appropriate. Worldwide COMMUNICATION – two-way, accurate, interactive CONNECTIVITY – an opportunity to use the right tool for the job.

quality product with total flexibility that will have the competitive edge.

Continuing success with CAD

Recently (1992–1993) the need for CAD was understood better by the clothing and textile industry. During the recession, businesses had to carefully manage their futures which resulted in investment in CAD to help secure a competitive edge. In turn, this has benefited the development of CAD since the expensive and time-consuming process of product design and development has been scrutinized again and again. The major influences of change have been:

- developments in computer and communication technology,
- acceptance of working with CAD as an everyday occurrence,
- the broadening of CAD investment, i.e. greater spread of businesses involved with systems tackling all aspects of the design and product development process.

This all results in:

- a shortage of skilled, CAD trained personnel.

CAD now provides us with an environment in which we can take the opportunity to challenge the conventional processes of market research, design, product development, product illustration and selection, and product information. This environment is dependent on investment, good management and access to the technology. We must envisage a future of the relevant computers on everyone's desk with personnel understanding how they are used to enhance their roles in the process.

To emphasise this new environment the diagram (Fig. 7.4) shows flexibility in process-order, extensive availability of CAD tools and the importance of communication and connectivity. Each business can develop as it sees appropriate.

The pitfalls of CAD

The possible pitfalls of CAD are synonymous with other major business technologies – *dependency*. So how do we avoid becoming vulnerable to issues like:

- de-skilling,
- insufficient initial and on-going training,
- working procedures with less personal contact,
- technology breaking down,
- managing new levels of data,
- security etc.?

The answers are mainly obvious but often very much overlooked when new methods of working are applied within a business and across the boundaries with their customers and suppliers. One of the major concerns is de-skilling. It is important to remember that CAD is a tool for an expert to enhance their specific part of the process and add to the overall success of the business. If we let the skills disappear, the technology will have little on which to base developments. On the other hand it is also necessary to recognise that new skills are developing with technology, and that even schoolchildren designing in 3D is already becoming commonplace.

Chapter 8
Practical Utilisation of CAD Systems in the Preparation, Creation and Processing of Designs for Textile Printing

CHARLES SHENEFIELD

Charles Shenefield has been in the printing industry for twenty-one years. The last thirteen of these in textile printing with the Tietex Corporation, where he is currently the Manager of the Engraving Department.

Introduction

The early CAD system of the 1970s brought a whole new way for textile companies to process designs. The possibility of totally filmless engraving encouraged some of the larger textile firms to embrace this new technology. The first systems were expensive, but they gave the companies that bought them an advantage. They were based on mainframe style computers that were state of the art when they were introduced, but as the PC improved, they were to be the platform of choice in the future.

PC based systems evolved for both weaving and printing of textile designs. Some specialised in one or the other and some were able to do both. The PC based systems were much less expensive so a large number of small- to medium-sized companies could join the growing movement to exploit technology's progress towards CAD/CAM technology.

It was at this time that my company began to evaluate CAD systems and what impact the purchase of one would have for us.

Evaluation of CAD systems

The evaluation of CAD systems is an important step before purchasing a system. All of the current CAD systems are able to process designs and so finding the one that will fit best with your company and the type of work, is not the easiest of tasks. Listed below are some of the major areas to consider when evaluating CAD systems:

(1) Total amount of budget for project.
(2) Number of designs expected to process per week.
(3) Size of designs to be processed.
(4) Input devices
    (a) Flat bed scanner
    (b) Drum scanner
(5) Editing software
    (a) Drawing functions
    (b) Colour reduction
    (c) Dot removal
    (d) Separation software
    (e) Tone processing
(6) Output device
    (a) Film plotters
    (b) Digital colour separation
    (c) Colour. Ink-jet printers.
(7) The number of designs that are expected to be processed per week will be important regarding what size of computers you will need and how many workstations are required to start with. The size of design will affect the type and size of both scanners and printers you will select, plus the skills of people to use the system. The editing software will make a difference as far as the type of design that will go through the system, both the easiest and the ones which will take longer. Also the way the software is used will determine how quickly new operators will become proficient on the system.

   The output devices will be chosen by how you intend to use the digital files after editing. Digital separation to drive a laser engraver, film plotting for exposing screens, ink-jet printer for proofing and customer approval of designs.

Uses of CAD systems

The main uses of CAD systems are the creation of original designs, or the interpretation of artwork supplied by customers. The latter being either painted artwork, fabric samples or possibly black and white film negatives which we have used on our CAD for all of the above reasons.

Most of the designs we have processed have been customer supplied artwork, with around 90% being painted artwork, 9% fabric samples – and the rest, films sent in by the customer. We also have done the occasional creation of original design on our CAD system, but this still continues to be a small part of designs that are processed on our CAD system.

Scanning artwork

I feel that the scan is the single most important step in the processing of a design on a CAD system. The quality of the scan has more to do with the total time taken to do a design than any other function of a CAD system. The actual editing of a design is the largest time block for the processing of a design and the scan has the biggest effect on that function than anything else. Any time spent trying to improve the scan file will take hours, if not days off the editing time of a design.

Of course, the better the quality of the artwork to be scanned, the better the scan file will be. Artwork that is not creased or wrinkled but will lay flat on either a flat bed or drum scanner will give much better results than a piece of artwork that is creased or wrinkled. You may be able to defocus the scanning head to remove these, but you risk not getting all of the details of the artwork.

Also the contrast of the colours in the artwork has a lot to do with the outcome of the final scan. The more contrast between the colour – the cleaner and sharper the scan will be. You will also get less of a halo around the colours and less mixture of the colours in the scan that will have to be edited out later.

I have done some scans of colour copies of fabric samples but have found the results to be far worse than scanning the actual fabric, and do not recommend this as an alternative to scanning fabric. Scanning fabric has some problems built into it, but with a few techniques it can be done properly. One of the problems is that the scanner wants to pick up the construction of the fabric while scanning. This may be avoided by defocusing the scanning head until it no longer picks up the weave of the fabric. A second problem is keeping the fabric in contact with the drum of the scanner during the scanning operation. You can either place a piece of clear acetate film over the fabric to keep it down, or glue the fabric to a piece of acetate and then mount it to the drum of the scanner. I prefer the latter, as it can be hard to mount the fabric to the drum without stretching and distorting the images on the fabric.

We also use our scanner to scan in black and white, artwork and separates. Sometimes we will do an outline of a fabric sample or a piece of artwork that has similar colours or stipple effects that the scanner would have trouble seeing. Then we scan the outline and instruct our artist to draw the technique back in with the design system. In many cases, it can be much quicker to redraw these designs in the system than to edit out all of the mixture of colours that the scan file would produce.

Lastly, we also scan separates in black and white film, and then merge them back into a coloured design in our design station. We do this mostly with our existing film design to make them available to our colouring station and eventually to produce digital colour separation to drive our laser engraver.

The editing of designs

The first step in editing a design is to take the scan file and do some colour reduction to get the file as close as possible to the final number of colours that the finished design will have. Some of this will be done by the colour reduction function in the CAD system, where the computer picks the next closest colour left in the palette to replace the colour to be discarded, or the artist operator chooses which colour they want to replace the colour being discarded. We usually do a few steps of the computer reduction taking anything from one to four colours out at a time and assessing the results. After that, you usually have to manually select the colour to be replaced as the colour palette gets smaller.

The next thing is to put the pattern into repeat. If the design was painted in repeat, it is just a matter of trimming the design into the proper size of the repeat. If it was not in repeat, the CAD system has many functions to help create a repeat in a design. You can add areas around the existing design and fill these areas by copying motifs from the original design. The use of clone brushes is helpful in the blending of wash effect and backgrounds into the new areas of the design or the artist can draw new motifs to complete the repeat. The main reason to put the design in repeat early in the processing is to eliminate the editing of areas on the scan file that will not be in the final design.

Following this is the cleaning up of individual images or motifs. Here we use a combination of reduce brushes, dot clear brushes, dot removal and drawing function. The ability to capture a motif and make it into a pattern is also very helpful. To pull it away from the design is a very powerful tool in the hand of a skilled operator. Finally the redrawing of the motif with one of the freehand lines and brushes to give the images the smoothness of the painted artwork.

At this stage, any tone work or mixes of colours are set up to create the final palette of the design. Both tone and mixes help a great deal in creation of the subtle effects required in most of the textile designs of today.

Colour work on CAD systems

We use our colouring station and our ink-jet printer in three different ways. First is for the proofing of designs in progress. At various stages of editing, ink-jet proofs of the design are produced for the computer artist and the stylist to go over and make decisions as to what still needs to be done to the design.

Secondly, full-size ink-jet proofs are made of the design for customer or product manager approval. This allows them to make comments or changes before any engraving is done.

Then lastly and most importantly, we use our colouring station for the creation of new colourways of patterns and for the customer's approval of these colourways before actual strike-offs are done on a fabric. We also use the colour chips generated by these printouts to develop colour formulas for our production lots.

Making separations with a CAD system

The ability of a CAD system to generate colour separations that give you all of the same options as traditional film separations is a very important function of any CAD system. The ability to create traps by either expanding or contracting colours is essential. Having the ability to have all of the colours in a design trap, every other colour in the design by different amounts is a feature which we use on a limited amount of separation sets, but not to be able to do that would severely limit our ability to be able to match the work we did before going to a CAD system. Also, the abilities to continue two or more colours on to a single separation is a function we use quite often.

How a system handles tone work is equally important where you are doing designs that have a water-colour look or for doing a pattern with a lot of subtle blending of colours. Being able to have some of the tones fall on solid colour or to platform tone together are some of the features we use to achieve the look of these types of design. The ability to output the tone of a design at a different resolution makes it possible to do very fine tone work. If you will be using these separations to drive a laser engraver that has tone generating capabilities, you can output your separation in a gray scale format and by so doing, reduce the size of those files.

Once the separations have been produced, there are two major ways of using them. One is to send these files to a film plotter to expose a film to use later to create a flat on a rotary screen. Secondly, you can use the digital separation to drive a laser engraving system to burn the design into a screen or printing cylinder. This is how we use digital separation that we generate on our CAD system. One of the benefits of purchasing our CAD system was to eliminate the making and use of films in our operation.

Artists and managing a CAD system

A few of the most important attitudes for a computer artist to have are: to be able to constantly adapt to new software and to be creative in the use of the functions provided. We found that a willingness to experiment with new combinations of functions has led to quite a few time-saving techniques. Also the keeping of notebooks with a history of how designs were processed was extremely helpful, as sometimes some functions or combinations of functions used to do one design might not be needed until a similar design comes up weeks or months later. The regular meeting and exchanging of ideas by all artists using the system is a strong tool for making the best use of any CAD system.

Conclusion

The changeover from traditional design work to using a CAD system can be a very positive experience. First, determine your needs. Select a CAD supplier who has the hardware and software to meet these needs. Also, one who will help you train your people in the basic use of their system and who will work with you to keep their system growing to meet your future needs. The support of the CAD supplier is paramount in the successful implementation of a CAD system into your company. Use bright creative people to operate and manage it and, where possible, form relations with other CAD users. A dialogue with other CAD users can expose you to new ways of using, and thinking about your CAD system, that you might not arrive at on your own.

In doing all of this, I think you will find that both the quality and quantity of your design work will improve and give a faster turn-around of designs, earlier customer involvement and the ability to produce new colourways. These are just a few of the positive effects that having a CAD system has brought to my company. I have no doubt that implementing a CAD system was the only way for our company to stay competitive in today's market place. Only with our continuing understanding of new ways of exploring those capabilities will we increase our customer's satisfaction in the future.

THE EDUCATORS

Chapter 9
Training and Education

JOHN HARVEY VALLENDER

John Harvey Vallender entered the bespoke clothing industry in 1967 and worked for fifteen years in a high class bespoke manufacturing retail organisation, specialising in pattern cutting. He entered the teaching profession in 1981; his specialism is pattern cutting and cutting room practice. He has cultivated an interest in information technology and computer aided design and machine management. He has become expert in the use of the Lectra CAD system in pattern development, grading and lay planning.

His industrial and professional qualifications include a full advanced certification in clothing technology, a Cert. Ed. and B.Ed. He has a particular interest in curriculum development and assessment. An accredited CBT (Computer Based Training) author and a member of the CFCI course review panel, he is committed to the fostering of industrial links with colleges. He is presently a lecturer at Handsworth College where he is also responsible for the provision of consultancy and bureau facilities.

Introduction

This chapter is intended for individuals who are developing learning materials for others, or for learners planning their own learning programmes in applied CAD. Its purpose is to share a number of ideas which may aid the process of learning to use CAD.

The chapter begins with a personal view of the nature of CAD systems, then considers some fundamental learning theories and attempts to link these to a possible learning process which may be employed for CAD. The chapter concludes by offering a simple description of a tested format for a CAD learning resource.

Let me start by making a general observation: 'learning is likely to be more successful if a learner appreciates the way in which CAD systems function'. This is not to say that a learner should have detailed technical knowledge of a system, but rather that they should possess a general overview of functions and limitations. When the learner knows what the functions are and is familiar with what can be achieved with a system, he or she is likely to be more efficient and effective when learning its use. (By system I mean an integrated set of component pieces of equipment and computer programs which have been collected together for a particular purpose.)

In other words, I am suggesting that successful learning is fostered if the learner approaches the task with a realistic conception of what can be done with a system and what to expect of it.

Computer systems have operational hierarchies and procedures, as do the software applications which are to run on them. These hierarchies are determined by the designers of the hardware and software. As a general rule, users of CAD systems do not have the authority or technical skills to change these hierarchies. Therefore potential learners are obliged to adopt, without amendment, the fundamental hierarchies, procedures and functions provided for them.

Put another way, a user has access to a hardware and software 'box of tools'. The tools included are arbitrary, any choice being associated with decisions on which tool to use. Users have to recognise and learn the primary function of each 'tool' and the correct way to use it. Failure to use a tool correctly will usually result in the system displaying an error message, and may in some cases cause the system to stop working ('crash'). Learning to use the tools is more to do with knowing that something operates and produces results rather than knowing how or why the tool is as it is. Only after learning the effect of pressing this key or that button in a certain sequence can a user begin to use a system for solving problems. Such learning must be accomplished before a user can exploit the latent potential of a system.

The powerful and exciting 'what happens if' nature of CAD is founded on a good vocational understanding of the problem to be solved, linked to and enhanced by appropriate use of the tools provided by the system.

The case so far is: the individual elements ('tools') available within a system are the property of the CAD system designers. The function of each tool must be learned without question, and once this has been achieved control moves from the designer of the system to the user. This occurs as the user begins to employ the tools in the system's toolbox in unique combinations.

A learning programme

This is an outline of a programme which the reader may consider adopting and modifying as a model for planning their own, or someone else's, learning of a CAD system. To assist a learner, a training manager must strictly and clearly determine initiation to a system. A manager must decide what is important for the learner to know, in what order this 'knowing' is to be acquired and how best to achieve it; in other words what curriculum needs to be planned.

To help in this, a training needs analysis should be considered. This should help to determine which of the tools in the CAD box the user needs to employ, and which are to be introduced and learned about first. It is a mistake to attempt to introduce the whole spectrum of tools in one programme. One of the most important features of training success in CAD and computing in general is for the learning process to provide success within realistic and relevant experience. A manager must protect a learner from being 'overdosed' and overwhelmed by 'the possible', and direct learning towards 'the appropriate'.

In an industrial environment the training need will be determined by a specific job/task description and will be directly related to a specific production process. In an educational environment the manager will need to select an appropriate production process or design problem to be solved, and this will form the basis for the job/task description.

The first step will be to learn about the selected tools to be used. The next step will be to provide examples and safe experiences which exercise and guide the learner in the application of these tools. The final step will be setting the learners free when they are confident enough to begin planning combinations and applications for themselves.

Thus the anticipated learning will at first be teacher centred, but as the programme progresses, the teacher's role will change to one of guide and then of resource. Conversely, the learner's role will at first be disciplined by the coherence of a strict subject matter, but gradually the learner will be expected to accept more responsibility for his or her own learning.

To achieve implementation of this programme, some thought

must be given to how best to promote learning, and this in turn leads to some consideration of learning theories.

Learning theories

Learning theories can be polarised: at one extreme there are 'behaviourist or connectionist' theorists, and at the other extreme 'cognitive or field cognition' theorists. The fundamental difference between the two stems from their perception of the nature of the learning processes that humans employ.

The behaviourist views learning as a process of links between a stimulus and the response generated by that stimulus. Learning is seen as some sort of reaction and is expressed as a series of inputs and outputs, i.e. if this stimulus is done then that response will follow. Learners can be encouraged and motivated to 'react' to a specific stimulus in an expected manner. Thus it can be said that learning has taken place when a predetermined stimulus is followed by the required response.

On the other hand, cognitive theorists place the learner at the centre of the learning process and see learning as being proactive – a process based on internal thinking and the ability to be aware of the context and surroundings of an event in such a way that responses are flexible and valid but not necessarily reliable.

A crude comparison of the two perceptions can be expressed as:

- Behavioural learning is *externally* influenced and is done *to* the learner.
- Cognitive learning is *internally* influenced and done *by* the learner.

The behaviourist view

Behaviourist theorists such as J.B. Watson (1878–1958) and E.L. Thorndike (1874–1949) propose that undirected learning is accomplished when a random response to a stimulus proves successful, and responses are reinforced and established as learned when a given response to a stimulus repeats its success. Thus unsuccessful responses will be abandoned whereas repeating successful responses produces the appropriate stimulus response (S-R) pattern.

The theory goes on to claim that the more often a successful S-R pattern is exercised, the stronger will be the likelihood that a specific stimulus will generate its partner response; and further, that the sooner a response is seen to be a satisfactory conclusion of an initiating stimulus, the more likely the response is to be linked to that stimulus.

Perhaps the most influential behavioural theorist is B.F. Skinner, who proposed several valuable conclusions for training managers to consider:

(1) Each step in the learning process should be short and should grow out of previously learned behaviour.
(2) In the early stages learning should be regularly rewarded, and at all stages should be carefully controlled by a schedule of continuous and/or intermittent reinforcement.
(3) Reward should follow quickly when a correct response appears.
(4) The learner should be given an opportunity to discover stimulus discriminations for the most likely path to success (D. Child 1981).

Skinner suggests a distinction from the reactive learning expressed by Watson and Thorndike; he prefers to view the S-R partnership as being generated by the learner as he operates on his environment. Where Skinner's theories prove less useful is in illuminating what is going on inside the learner during the learning process. His work is essentially to do with the observable, external manifestations of learning. Skinner's conclusions about learning could well suit instructional type objectives, such as listing, stating, repeating and, for our purposes, some of the key pressing activities required of CAD.

Cognitive views

What seems to be missing are answers to some questions about meaning. What does learning mean to the individual? Surely there is more to human learning than can be explained by arrangements of S-R links. How is it that learners respond in different ways to the same stimulus? Cognition theorists argue that learners interact with a stimulus and that the response given is influenced by the learner's perception of an event, such learning is much more than a programmable response. The interaction is based on past experience and an understanding of the problem to be solved.

Founder members of the cognitivists movement were Köhler and Koffka; their particular school of psychology is known as 'gestalt' psychology. Perhaps their single most important contribution was their description of 'insight' as part of the process of learning, proposing that learning occurs when a solution to a problem is identified.

That is to say a response to a stimulus occurs suddenly as the learner perceives the whole problem and is able to reorganise the elements of the problem by restructuring his fields of perception in order to determine a probable solution.

The emphasis in gestalt psychology is adaptability; learning is formed from and based on existing knowledge and experience, which is modified to accommodate new perceptions and understanding. In this way learners progress from a low level to higher levels in a continuous spiral of increasing understanding and knowledge.

The learning process

Although not fully explored, it should be apparent that no one theory provides all the answers to the process of learning. In practice the most justifiable approach seems to be to use that which appears to be appropriate in any given situation.

A summary of the theories suggests that learning does take place when a response satisfies a stimulus, and that events which occur close together and are repeated tend to be learned more permanently. Also, learning occurs when a problem is seen as a whole and the relationships between the parts and the whole are restructured in context, using the resident knowledge of the learner as a base for progress and accommodation.

Put another way, it seems that successful learning can be achieved without recourse to understanding, but equally that learning can also be achieved through logical analysis which is dependent on understanding.

If this is true, is it useful to distinguish between these two apparent types of learning? If designers of curricula can recognise specific value and application in both types of learning – learning without understanding and learning based on understanding – then it follows that a curriculum should employ, encourage and exercise appropriate types of learning as required.

Take for example the initiation phase mentioned earlier. Learners may need to connect the various parts of the system and what happens when they press certain keys (in other words build S-R links). Later they will need to link series of key strokes as a procedure.

Questions to be answered at this early development stage are: Do the learners need to know why a key press generates a specific response? Or do they need to know which keys to press to achieve a required response? I would suggest that initially it is the latter. Therefore a manager may need to develop a learning resource which is initially designed to facilitate a strong behavioural S-R approach, in order to establish a 'habit' of key strokes.

However, once initiation has been achieved and the knowledge it represents has been established, the learning resource can move on to proposing and testing hypotheses based on problems and the tools currently available. The learning resource will therefore begin by employing S-R tactics and will quickly move towards employing learning strategies which rely on understanding and meaning. The first part of the resource will seek to provide models of S-R relationships and give opportunities for learners to practise these relationships, the learning being supported by clear product oriented assessment, which to a large extent can be self-assessment. In other words, learners will be told what happens when certain keys are pressed, stimulated to press these keys and rewarded for their success. Failure to secure the required response will initiate a remedial loop which will be followed with limited variation until the required S-R pattern is established.

The remainder of the resource will seek to establish cognitive learning associated with creative, analytical and evaluative thought. Having learned by rote that this or that key produces a specific response, the learners have to begin to plan how to link key presses in order to achieve specific ends. They have to begin to develop and use cognitive maps in order to construct efficient and effective strategies, otherwise their learning is unlikely to progress past the lowest level of trial and error.

The Piaget model of learning

Jean Piaget, a Swiss psychologist (1896–1980) proposed a model of learning which seems to be particularly useful for designers of curricula where cognitive processes dominate. Piaget's model was developed from a study of the development of childhood intellect, but the insight it gives to this branch of cognition is no less valuable in the development of CAD knowledge for adults.

Piaget proposes that 'real thinking is logical and follows the rules of logic'. Thus the goal of learning to use CAD is seen as a move from a situation where the environment, the computer's own hierarchy in this case, is overwhelmingly in control, to a situation where thought processes respond to the logic of the situation and judgements are based on the logical relationships between the CAD system and the problem to be solved.

The first stage towards developing this control begins with the successful interpretation of symbols: a system symbol becomes 'owned' by the learner in that the symbol holds personal meaning for the learner. Piaget suggests that such ownership is facilitated by the mode of imitation. Thus practice is vital to the successful construction of the logical learning sets that a learner uses to deal with a situation. (Piaget calls these systematic and co-ordinated learning sets 'schema'.) Piaget put forward the proposal that learners change their current learning sets in order to accommodate new knowledge, and that if the new knowledge is too far removed from their 'base' schema, learning is unlikely to occur. (A learner will try to know and understand a new situation by comparing it with what is already known and understood.)

Any changes to the schema are assimilated by the learner during inventive and imitative practice. Once accommodated and assimilated, revised schema can be used in similar situations of logic in the future. A learner literally builds his own knowledge by this accommodation and assimilation process. The implication for designers of learning materials must be that a careful progression of experiences should be provided which take the learner from where he is to a higher level of understanding and knowledge.

With understanding it is possible for a learner to recognise how a sequence of events leads to a conclusion, so when the learner is presented with a similar problem he can use his knowledge to think back from the current problem and propose solutions based on a previously tested schema. Thus design analysis and strategic planning are more firmly based on the probable than the possible.

The implication of this model is that learners should be challenged with problems that contain familiar elements, but that the elements should be presented in novel ways. In terms of designing a learning resource intended to develop knowledge, Piaget and fellow cognitivists' ideas can be expressed as: A learning resource should help the learner to:

(1) become aware of a problem;
(2) clarify the problem;
(3) propose hypotheses for the solution of the problem;
(4) reason out the implications of the hypotheses;
(5) test the problem against experience.

Put another way, development of knowledge is about interacting with the problems of the environment by applying to each problem a scientific and logical method of intelligent enquiry. Specifically for CAD the learning resource should be designed to:

(1) initiate the learner into the rules of a CAD system;
(2) demonstrate and provide practice in fundamental CAD procedures;
(3) demonstrate and provide practice in design analysis;
(4) demonstrate and encourage logical planning in the use of CAD simulation;
(5) encourage experimentation based on planning execution and evaluation of CAD simulations for vocational problems.

Model for learning CAD

It should be clear by now that I subscribe to the view that, for the most part, learning is something that the learner has to do. Therefore a learning resource should be designed to help the learner learn, rather than to teach to the learner – a resource which is capable of establishing specific and general rules in an efficient and informative fashion, but flexible enough to allow for knowledge to be understood in an efficient but personally relevant and meaningful way.

In other words the model will be essentially 'learner centred', by which I mean much more than the learner working at his own pace and being able to pick and choose entry points based on his prior experience. Learner centred in this case means a resource written with the learner first and the content second. The resource is expected to:

- provide initiation to predetermined procedures;
- provide opportunities for practice and reflection;
- provide opportunities for negotiating exercise material which is relevant to the learner;
- encourage logical planning;
- be flexible enough to allow learners with different and or low/high levels of experience to plan their own learning strategy.

Such a resource may be expected to open with a brief description of the CAD application to be used and the CAD system itself, and then transfer quickly into the initiation phase. The amount of new information at each stage will be kept to a minimum and each piece of information or practice builds on the previous one(s). In the early stages the learner will be given a description of what to expect and will be invited to imitate the activity being discussed (i.e. establishing S-R partnerships). Later the learner will be presented with a more complex series of procedures and will again be invited to imitate using prepared sequences in the form of algorithms. Finally, the learner will be given a number of design problems to solve (i.e. establishing new schema by accommodation and assimilation).

Assessment of learning at this stage can be based on self and/or peer group. At the end of each stage a summary of activities should be given and at the end of the work an appendix of procedures may need to be provided as a quick reference. Consider using the first person, and keep computer jargon reduced to the essential. Too much jargon could exclude some learners. Wherever possible, assessment should be based on real and negotiated problems intended to facilitate and demonstrate that assimilation of CAD concepts and CAD practice has taken place.

Conclusion

This chapter has attempted to outline and justify a design process of a learning resource for CAD. It has looked at learning theory and recommended that a pragmatic approach should be adopted, where learning is seen as an activity of the learner accommodating and assimilating knowledge in a meaningful way. The 'teacher' is seen as a helper in this process.

It is important to re-state that the central function of the learning resource is to develop CAD thinking. As Jerome Bruner (1960), quoted by Dennis Child, put it: 'methods of inquiry are more durable than facts and even generalisations'. It is the students who have to learn, and they will do so best by interacting with their environment. Therefore to be helpful the resource will have to 'arrange' events in such a way that learners are encouraged to interact productively with, in this case, the CAD system being used. David Ausubel (1969), also quoted by Dennis Child, uses the term 'advanced organisers' to describe this activity.

To summarise, learning is something that learners have to do for themselves. In the first instance they have to learn what tools are available and what each tool does. They then have to discover, in a purposeful and directed way, how to use CAD – to develop an enquiring attitude towards the use of CAD in simulated solutions to vocationally oriented design problems.

Such discovery learning tends to imply learning based on the individual or on small group activity. Therefore the learning resource should in its latter stages permit individualistic learning without absolutely requiring it. Because, for most learners, CAD will be a new experience, the resource or package as it will now be called will need to facilitate a progression from teacher centred subject initiation thought to student centred hypothesising and evaluation. To execute this change the package must enable learners to shape and use the ideas being developed, in such a way that the learner contributes, applies, tests and evaluates the activities promoted by the package. In other words, it is essential that the learner constructs his or her own meaningful interaction using his/her own store of experience as the basis for extending knowledge and understanding. In practice this means allowing the learner to provide his/her own focus for learning and assessment problems.

A basic introduction to the learning theories discussed in this chapter can be found in the book by Denis Child, noted in the reading list below.

Suggested Reading List

Anderson D.C. (1981)　　Evaluating Curriculum Proposals.
Croom Helm, London.

British Gas (1986)　　A systems approach to training.
Futuremedia Ltd, Bognor Regis.

Child D. (1981)　　Psychology and the Teacher.
Holt, Rinehart & Winston Ltd,
Eastbourne.

Further Education Unit (1981)　　Curriculum Change – an evaluation of
TEC programme development in
colleges.
Department of Education & Science,
Stanmore.

Further Education Unit (1988)　　The Key Technologies – some
implications for education and training.
Department of Education & Science,
Stanmore.

Further Education Unit (1989)　　The Concept of Key Technologies.
Department of Education & Science,
Stanmore.

Lee, D. (1975)   The Doris Lee Lectures – Curriculum.
                              University of London Institute of
                              Education, London.

Heathcote G. et al. (1980)   Integration or co-ordination.
                              NATFHE Journal, Feb 1980.

McNally D.W. (1977)   Piaget, Education and Teaching.
                              The Harvester Press Ltd, Hassocks.

O'Hear A. (1981)   Education Society and Human Nature.
                              Routledge & Kegan Paul, London.

Peters R.S. (1971)   Ethics and Education.
                              Allen Unwin, London.

Rowntree D. (1974)   Educational technology in curriculum
                              development.
                              Harper Row, London.

Sockett H. (1976)   Designing the curriculum.
                              Open Books, London.

Warwick D. (1987)   The Modular Curriculum.
                              Basil Blackwell Ltd, Oxford.

Chapter 10
Training and Education in CAD Clothing/Textiles Systems

JANE DEVANE

Jane Devane graduated from Cheltenham School of Art & Design with a First Class Honours Degree in Fine Art and gained a Master's Degree at the Royal College of Art, London. She received a Fellowship from North West Arts and was the Artist in Residence at Crewe and Alsager College of Higher Education. Jane Devane is joint course leader and Field Chair designate in fashion at Cheltenham and Gloucester College of Higher Education, and is currently helping to develop a new BA Hons Modular Degree course in Fashion Design Technology, subject to validation in 1994.

Introduction

As a practising artist and current course leader on a National Diploma course in fashion at Cheltenham and Gloucester College of Higher Education, I have welcomed the increased opportunity to explore the use of CAD in education. I am mainly concerned with textile design, fashion illustration and visual studies which combine basic design, drawing and colour. All these subjects are concerned with image making and so the introduction of computer graphics has had a strong impact on design education. It has generated the need for artists and designers like myself to understand, adapt and support the integration of various computer systems into the educational programme, and I feel strongly that good design courses need to take full advantage of this new form of visual communication.

For the last two years most of the students who have applied for a place on the Fashion Diploma Course have come equipped with basic computer experience. They may have started with an Amstrad at home for word processing and spreadsheets for numerical and textual analysis and then at school have been encouraged to look at the creative ways in which computers are used in the classroom. I have found that these novice fashion students already begin to think in different ways; they appear to rely more on each other and themselves to gain information and seem less dependent on the traditional tutor/student role. They are self motivated and anxious to take on board the technological advances being made within the fashion industry. Their enthusiasm to experience and research with CAD regarding fashion and textiles is amazing. They possess a very positive attitude to the present systems incorporated into our educational programme and within a short time can handle the most sophisticated equipment with great dexterity.

I am also a tutor for the Higher National Diploma course in Fashion Design Technology at the same college. As the course title suggests, it is a course of study for creative people with a preference for practical skills and a strong interest in fashion technology. Computer creativity has replaced the 'programming' of sequences to design systems rather than just using standard utilities. The course was planned as a direct reply to the current needs of the fashion industry. As this is the first of a new and still rare kind of course – bridging the gap between creative design and fashion design technology – the use of computers in the different areas of the fashion industry forms the backbone of this course. Computers are its speciality and all students gain integrated knowledge of computer literacy during their two years of study.

Both Diploma and Higher National Diploma courses encourage students to use the well-equipped computer workshops to study colour, fashion graphics and textile design. The CAD projects set vary enormously from straightforward colour exercises and experimentation to work with video images for illustration and even to the construction of a three-dimensional object made from actual computer printouts.

There is also a cluster of terminals for general information technology etc. Our Design students acquire and develop basic business skills through the use of writing tools, numerical analysis, spreadsheets, graphs, display tools etc. The collection of data and its application in the Fashion environment has enabled students to explore other career paths such as supervisors, managers, being self-employed. We also see our students employed as pattern cutter/designers, computer operators/demonstrators in design rooms and computer companies, or as graders, lay-planners and designer/illustrators using CAD, and as designer/technologists for computer software companies requiring fashion expertise.

As new roles are created within the industry because of the increased use of computers for diverse functions, the potential employment market is growing rapidly worldwide. Final year students have found it easy to gain employment because the necessary computer experience was built into their work at college. One student recently produced an optical database with an historical context for designers and fashion forecasters, to enable them to make effective and useful design research. She worked in collaboration with Moda CAD and other CAD/CAM companies to assess current computer aided design systems. This same student will receive a research bursary to study and specialise in this area in greater depth. Another student for her final major project produced a computer made to measure grading system targeted towards the marketing of clothes for physically disabled children. This innovative idea won the student a major award from the British Association of Clothing Machinery Manufacturers in 1993.

Students studying the HND course can specialise in one aspect of the course during their last year. They can either work with an individual sponsor or gain additional work experience. Several students decided to specialise within the area of CAD and chose to explore pattern grading. With consultation from industry they compared the traditional methods and the advances being made with the impact of computer technology. Various computer systems were compared. Another student compared the traditional system and the Ormus PDS system both in pattern cutting and grading methods. Both students have gained subsequent employment within the fashion industry.

Integration in education

The recently changing attitudes of designers and artists towards CAD, and in particular its contribution to art and fashion education, have given birth to a new visual language whose creative, innovative and stimulating work can no longer be ignored. A new breed of fashion/textile student is beginning to emerge. CAD/CAM is no longer a vision; it is reality in the fashion industry and therefore there have been changes and efforts made to incorporate the introduction of this technology and its far reaching implications into education. I am now optimistic about this integration having seen the results and the potential, but to begin with I had several reservations.

I, like many others from a traditional Fine Art background, anticipated the technological advances in design education. However, I saw them independently and definitely outside the studio environment. Unfamiliarity with computer systems, the jargon and the medium led to an ignorance and distrust of their use – whatever that was. I did not wish to question or explore the seemingly complex functions of this sophisticated equipment which was always then housed in a sterile office environment. My reaction was to protest against any 'hands on' experience regarding my own work and I hesitated to employ any computer system when teaching or introducing drawing and textile projects to my fashion students. Nevertheless, as new systems were operated by these students with great success, I became aware of good things beginning to emerge. There were definite improvements in their presentation and illustration. The work they produced reflected an obvious interest and enjoyment. Their designs were creative, expressive and varied; problematic drawing skills had been overcome. If the students had given their approval for using computers in all subject areas, then it was time to find out why.

My initial approach to so-called 'economically efficient' workstations proved to be less daunting than I had first imagined. During a short period of staff development I started coming to terms with a Zenith, Paint Box and Cameo Paint. I was encouraged to ignore the lengthy and explicit manuals, ease of use being a priority. Words like pixel, menus, palettes, stylus or mouse were absorbed and then forgotten. Clever and creative designs evolved from a host of mistakes and wrong instructions.

With very little effort on my part the computer guided me through a considerable range of colours, effects and designs with a few clicks of the electronic pen. Within a short time I was able to experiment with various brush types, washes, pencils and chalk. Then it was on to flood filling, image merging and zoom functions, adding to the long list of impressive features. I came away thinking how easy it all was. I also became aware that having previously known nothing about computers and then sharing this learning experience with my students, a better working relationship resulted. Discussions on various software, the problems that face a computer-illiterate person, the embarrassments of drawing with a mouse and other relevant exchanges of information proved to be excellent therapy.

Differences in the medium

It was of course very different from holding a pencil on a piece of paper. I missed the feel of the texture of paper or canvas, the absorption of the paint or washes and the physical pleasure of creating an exciting surface or design with layers of chalk, wax, paint and collage. The spontaneous accident or mess found in the artist's studio, from which an interesting and original design might emerge, was impossible. I feel that surface texture and tactile materials are very important to a textile designer. Although it is now possible to texture map, taking a surface texture from a photograph and mapping it on to an image, this clever technique can only heighten realism on the screen, nothing more. Regarding drawing, students will always need to acquire the formal skills and sensitivity of practice from a drawing studio before they have access to the computer. The free-hand computer sketching ability can only reflect the students' own skills and general drawing ability.

One of the most frustrating limitations of any computer painting system is the actual size of work produced. I work on a large scale and therefore felt it necessary to manipulate small computer printouts using collage, repetition and other techniques. I have also encouraged students to think in terms of three dimensions on a large scale, whereby sculpture and weaving for instance with printouts can become an attractive and stimulating possibility. This manipulation and adaptation of CAD and its characteristics can be a fascinating area to explore. The results can be very interesting and can help to counterbalance the disadvantages of this complex technology and break down the barriers that exist between the creative arts and the so-called 'technology of science'.

Another problem is the screen. To sit for a long time in front of a screen that is only 10 in across its diagonal, fighting against the reflection of light, is not really conducive to producing good quality work. If you have 16 million colours it is vital to have a screen that can support them; no one wants a monochrome screen for CAD work.

It is useful to have a back-up of the screen in the memory, so that if you make a complete mess of something you can go back one step. If you have a good screen and a fast computer you do not want to use a keyboard to check designs. A mouse is not a suitable tool for good CAD; a graphic tablet and stylus is more appropriate.

Most of the computer art I have seen in recent exhibitions has shown some amazing images and ranges of visual effects. Whether or not this work has real artistic qualities is debatable. Artists who have decided to work with computers seem very intent on creating images that cannot be achieved by other means. They make use of the

computer 'uniqueness'. Fantasy and reality often combine to produce exciting images. Pictures can be made with light instead of paint – the work of a computer scientist rather than an artist. It is all very advanced and reflects developments of image technology, but there is very little work where an artist has used the computer to produce drawn images that portray observations and an interest in subject matter around them.

When I decided to use the computer as a tool to create a new dimension to my own work, I realised that technical support is a must. Computers do amazing things but they need instructions and logical operations. Short introductory courses regarding their basic components and functions are a must. Although this basic theory can appear to be complex at first, one does not need a degree in mathematics to acquire the appropriate skills. Some students have said they would like to learn how to program a computer, so it will perform functions they might require of it. In my attempts to use CAD in my own work I soon realised how a computer can dictate, and that what one may have originally intended can suddenly change; you need little or no aesthetic sensibility to create a wide range of patterns and designs.

This is a problem, particularly in the training of students. They can easily let the computer interfere and impose its own structures on their images, which can make assessment and critical appraisal very difficult. In several projects I have found it hard to extract what the computer did and what the student intended it to do. The sheer quantity of work that can be produced by one student in a short time can also be a disadvantage as well as an advantage. The speed and the ability to accomplish a routine task such as experimentation of different colourways or to eradicate paint or mistakes very easily, do not have any relevance from a fine art stance but from a fashion or textile point of view perhaps they do. However, as a piece of equipment that can help create an image, store and manipulate it, the benefits for any creative person, fine artist or fashion student, are obvious.

CAD in fashion/textile courses

As the machines become more user friendly and easier to use, there is a need to concentrate on how students in fashion/textile design use them. The electronic systems work well as a creative medium in design education and they can portray what has been visualised imaginatively by any student, but students must be encouraged to adapt this technology to serve their own creative requirements.

The systems are not merely more complex but obviously very different from the conventional creative tools found in a stimulating college environment. It is now possible to combine photography, cinematography, painting and drawing into one. But with this amazing box of tricks I find the students are usually loath to do any more to their computer creations. They see them as final statements or solutions that have been arrived at by complex exercises. However, in my projects I encourage them to photocopy, tear, enlarge, pleat, fold, work over these images using and incorporating other techniques, so that the progression of design development can continue and be seen as ongoing practice.

I feel very strongly that students should see CAD as an important accessory to other work. When I give a textile project to a group of students, the preparatory research, observations, drawings and experimental designs all exhibit very strong individual characteristics. When these are fed into the computer for further development, the results from the same group of students often appear to be very similar and repetitive. Obviously some students may have a preference for subtle colour while others prefer strong tonal contrasts. Most of the students will have taken advantage of repeat pattern, creating minor images and using 'cut and paste', but individual interpretation of ideas does seem lacking. Perhaps much of the sameness arises due to the fact that the students watch others manipulating the computer system in order to be familiar with the routine, rather than find pathways of knowledge on their own. It is only when this work is taken back to the studio for each student to reanalyse and refine his or her designs, that the work finally produced reflects individual intention and responses. Each student's creative ability can then be seen and assessed. If the use of the computer and its sequence of buttons to press takes precedence over individual creativity then those who design computer systems must be aware and understand their uses, requirements ability and have knowledge of the students' subject.

Most of the computer systems we have at college vary in price and performance but we do have a wide range of programs essential for CAD and computer graphics. Finding the space to accommodate this equipment and allowing access to large groups of students from many departments is a constant problem. We have recently adopted a booking system and a flexible timetable as a solution to the problem of demand and overcrowding. More importantly, we have full-time technical support, and the expert service they provide is invaluable.

Integrated projects, whereby fashion students can work in the photography and audio visual departments, are encouraged and the work they can create with the aid of computers allows these students to work frequently with high-technology media.

Choice of equipment

The question of which computers should be purchased for the training and education of CAD for fashion and textile students is not really necessary; the real question is 'What do I want to do and how can a computer help me do it?'. A computer expert and a designer want different things. How computers are used in industry may differ from how they are used in education, and the different needs and requests must be met separately.

As far as the computer industry is concerned speed is of the essence, but this is not a priority in education. Designers must use full colour even if they only have access to a nine pin dot matrix printer fitted with black ribbon cartridge. Designers are very rarely able to say what they want in terms of hardware. However, they do say that they would like to use a variety of brushes and drawing tools, to have a choice of colours from a large palette, to be able to erase easily, to block fill areas and draw smooth curves or generate squares and rectangles, and to make pure areas and create freehand shapes; the software range available for CAD is almost endless. It is important to have someone within the fashion department who knows what is required and can make sure the purchase of equipment will meet the demands of a fashion department and cater to the individual needs of a designer.

Our lecturer in Design Computing has said that if he had an unlimited budget, he would build 'a system that comprised an "invisible" computer with an upgradeable processor, and a video bus with its own high speed processing. A graphics card capable of supporting 1280*1024 pixels on a large, flicker free screen. The graphic tablet would be A0 and have a pressure sensitive, cordless stylus. A quality A3 colour scanner comes without saying. Interfaces should include video and CD-ROM controllers including multimedia support. Because of the size of the files being generated a high speed, read/write optical disk becomes essential. Output direct to a colour copier with an intelligent processing unit should solve some of the usual printing problems, and provide hard copy output up to A0 albeit tiled from A3. On an A0 colour ink-jet printer could be used.

Colour matching is imperative. There is a wide range of software available for designers and a mixture of packages would be selected. A good presentation package for on-screen still and video productions could be used creatively. Just to complete the system, a digital video camera should just about see off any loose change!'

With a restricted budget in education, providing the resources for CAD and its development will always be under constant negotiation and supervision. The introduction of CAD means fundamental changes in finance, perhaps with sponsorship from computer manu-facturers likely in order that a progressive fashion course can keep up with the technological advances made. From design and creation to management of these elements – the building up of a library to designs and elements of designs. The place for this is in the com-mercial world. Such databases will consist of illustrations, text and numbers. Investment is needed by colleges to provide such tool kits for students to experiment with. The bringing together of files of data production.

The uses in education

Teaching is a two-way dialogue, an active and responsive endeavour. Listening to students' concerns, attitudes and questions about CAD, its practices and complexities has helped to develop new approaches to teaching and learning. The following are a selection of comments from present Fashion students from Cheltenham and Gloucester College of Higher Education, who see the computer as a tool and an integral part of their work, and not as a specialist subject area:

I chose this course because of the different approach that it offered. Computers are a very important part of the fashion industry and all educational centres that address Fashion should be using them.'

'I find that using computers helps me to present my ideas clearly and professionally. I can add colour, texture and fabric suggestions to my design work, and incorporate this without great difficulty as part of the design process. However, I do think that those who design the equipment should look at improving the stylus to make it more accurate.'

'Computers are an invaluable aid to students, who like myself find presentation difficult. They open up a whole new area to explore and experiment with, which in turn gives the user confidence and the necessary skills to develop and work ideas through.'

'I find that computers enable me to present my work to a professional standard. I do enjoy using them and find the results rewarding. However, I feel that they must be housed in a design studio and not in an 'office environment' so that their use is promoted as part of the design process, rather than an extra activity. They can then be more 'user friendly' and possibly used more creatively.'

'Computers save time and enable one to create and present ideas if you can use the tools properly. Personally I am not technically minded and find them quite difficult to use. Technical support and simple manuals must be available together with help on a one-to-one basis.'

Conclusion

I believe that to provide effectively the necessary computer technology required in a learning environment, information technology must enable fashion students to realise the applications, become familiar with the benefits and examine how they wish to use CAD as a medium. Our students are encouraged to question the use of computers and to evaluate when they should and should not be applied. They are made aware of this technology's potential and understand the advantages and disadvantages, but also realise that although each fashion course places a certain emphasis on the use of computers, it is not at the expense of traditional skills.

As a lecturer who works with a team, it is my role to nurture the understanding of colour, texture, shape and composition. The use of traditional drawing methods to strengthen visual awareness and encourage drawing for selection and visual information, play a key role in the development of each student's thinking within a fashion and textile context. The processes then help to build the visual vocabulary, and the exchange of opinions and ideas is the basic prerequisite of all artists and designers; the end product is an accumulation of all the processes and therefore not an end in itself. All this has been and can be achieved without the use of any computer system. However, there is no one way to develop the necessary skills and sensibilities required to create and design; therefore the introduction of CAD for experimentation and innovation can at the very least provide another alternative. As long as the focus of attention is on the quality of ideas and work, the aesthetic and design aspect of any fashion and textile course can be allowed to progress.

It is obvious the computers can contribute positively to design education. They are a medium through which personal creativity and originality can be enhanced and expressed. Their varied functions provide a platform from which to explore many exciting new areas that can stimulate and challenge an enquiring mind. Their speed is motivating because it allows a student to examine infinite alternatives before making a final design decision. In common with progressive elements in all areas of industrial development, this universal assistance of info-tech is an essential requirement.

However, the loss of some acquired skills through manual experience is bound to be a factor against sole computer design. This new technology must be seen as an instrument of assistance rather than a replacement technique. Imagination, initiative and intuitive response can be found and nurtured in any student but cannot as yet be found in any computer. The lack of interactive discussion between the user and the machine and the even greater lack of sensory facilities suggests that CAD has a long way to go yet. Only time and experience will indicate the limits to which CAD can be accepted.

Acknowledgements

Alan Villaweaver, Head of GCAM at Cheltenham and Gloucester College of Higher Education.

Sandre Jeans, Senior Associate Lecturer in Information Technology and Business Consultant at Cheltenham and Gloucester College of Higher Education.

Chapter 11
Teaching Clothing Design by Computer Aided Design: Aspirations and Realities

WINIFRED ALDRICH

Winifred Aldrich is a practising designer, experienced in both industry and education, and now working in computer aided design at the Nottingham Fashion Centre. She was previously a lecturer in Loughborough and London in clothing design and pattern cutting and has published three books on the subject. She completed her Ph.D in CAD in clothing design at the Nottingham Trent University in 1990, where she is continuing her research in this field.

Introduction

It is often assumed that a college or university department is a collective culture with common aims, but the art and design departments are usually staffed by creative people with a strong sense of individualism whose interpretation of 'the common aims' may differ radically. The pressure from authoritative bodies to include CAD into the curriculum of textile and clothing courses, when many staff have had no means of developing their own individual attitudes towards the phenomena (three-day crash courses are very often counterproductive), has presented a number of problems to Fashion and Clothing departments. Some departments may have a philosophical position that is opposed to its inclusion into the course. There may be conflicting views within a department. Other departments may be enthusiastic about its admission, but their staff may also be overburdened by workloads and increasing student numbers, leaving little time to develop their skills to the competence required for teaching a complex body of knowledge. One approach is to take the teaching of

CAD knowledge out of the department and offer it as a CAD module under the supervision of Computer Studies staff.

Curriculum planning can become dominated by the logistics of resources. Any planning of a curriculum innovation should be confronted by the educational considerations and an assessment of the quality of the learning experience which will be offered to each *individual* student.

An opportunity occurred to examine some of these issues in a research project which looked at different approaches to including CAD in pattern cutting and development. Every teaching experience differs, its participants and context are subject to external aims and controls. This chapter is not intended to be in any way prescriptive, it is a description of the events of the study. Substantial sections are devoted to students' views, and this may help colleges and universities in the process of introducing CAD, to understand possible outcomes when implementing what appears to be simple directives from Working Parties and the Responsible Bodies.

'Courses in Art and Design *should* therefore include at an early stage effective means of demonstrating to students the importance of IT in the area of their likely professional activity, and its relationship to the traditional component of Art and Design courses.'[1]

'it *should be* the policy of institutions to make specific resource provision for IT related developments. . . .'[2]

'Incorporation of information technology into the content of a design course *requires curriculum* re-design. *IT cannot adequately be achieved just by* adding on another module.'[3]

Background to a curriculum project

An earlier study of students using CAD[4], which looked at students' views of its use, found that a range of attitudes appeared to be significantly related to their individual needs and aspirations.

One of the principal findings of this study was that the students' modes of thought and their approach to design differed. They often conflicted with the conventional methods of pattern cutting and design procedures that they had experienced at the beginning and during their course. Some found areas of CAD more intelligible and compatible with their thought processes, mode of intelligence and perception. An understanding of the value of CAD as part of the process of acquiring knowledge of pattern cutting was unresolved by the study.

However, the findings of this earlier study offered sufficient confidence to undertake a curriculum project in which, instead of CAD being offered as a supplement to a teaching programme, it became integrated into the initial training module for design and pattern cutting. The module was part of the first year of a four year BA Hons. Clothing with Textiles course (the third year of which is an industrial placement). The participants were six first year students, they were selected by drawing lots from the high percentage (78%) who had expressed an interest. The group was reduced to five as one student was transferred to another University because of family commitments.

The students followed the same syllabus as the remaining main group of forty-eight students. The pattern cutting module in the first year required the design and pattern construction of a shirt. The module (10 weeks) was designed to demonstrate to students the processes required to develop an idea through to the working specifications required to manufacture the product. The project was used as a vehicle to develop knowledge of basic terms and procedures. The same limits, tutor contact, and studio time operated for both groups of students. After the first term the five students rejoined the main group, the following year their pattern cutting module, by manual methods, was taken with the main group. However, the main group's experience of CAD pattern technology was designed as an 'add on' module at the end of their second year. The responsibility for this work was taken by a tutor of Computer Studies.

The initial pattern cutting experience was taught to the five research group students in a design studio where CAD systems were available when required, but workbench areas and dress stands were as readily available. The students were taught through the media of CAD wherever it was thought applicable, and this was found to be approximately 70% of the module. Introduction to the body form took place on the dress stand with a garment being modelled. This was a duplication of the initial learning experiences of the main group.

At the end of the second year the research students, students from the main group and the tutors were interviewed and they discussed their experiences.

The purpose of the study was, first, to assess if it was *possible* in a believed 'ideal situation' to teach students the practical skills and knowledge of design and pattern cutting concurrently with knowledge of CAD; second, to assess if there may be any differences if students were offered knowledge in this manner, and third to look at any effects of 'add on' computer modules.

The findings of the study

The findings were considered in three areas; first, the previous skills, the previous assumptions of CAD within the research group (RGstudents) and a sample of five students from the main group (MGstudents). Second, a comparison of each group's experiences of CAD and pattern development during the two years of their course and their evaluations of their experiences; third, the tutors' evaluations of CAD instruction within the course.

Students' priorities are usually concerned with their current work. The earlier study[5] which looked at attitudes to CAD found this to be so. The students often have a heavy workload in short teaching terms of ten weeks. All the observation that took place, was of 'marked units' which counted towards the students' final degree and student motivation on the course did not appear to be a significant problem.

Previous skills and assumptions of the students

The two groups that were compared were very similar in character, both groups had two students with previous pattern cutting experience to BTEC level, three students in each group had word processing experience and one student had a little graphic experience. All of the students declared an early ignorance of the computer's use and capabilities in design and pattern development. Two RGstudents expressed a previous 'hatred' of computers, one 'couldn't understand why she had volunteered', the other saw it as an unfortunate necessity that would be good for her career.

The research group: Comparisons of two pattern cutting experiences

Pattern cutting with CAD

All five students were enthusiastic about their experiences and enjoyed working on the computer; some immediately, 'I liked working on it right from the beginning', others were surprised that they could master it. The students persevered until they could use it effectively.

They recognised that 'it takes a lot of practice before you can concentrate on the work instead of the operations of the computer'. Two of the students were Chinese, and one of them understood only a little English. These students diligently practised in their own time to overcome any difficulties.

Although all the students started with some form of shirt block, their methods of pattern adaptation differed. Two of the students preferred to work in a holistic way with all their pattern pieces on screen, they were not concerned with final accuracy until they had experimented with the shapes. Three students preferred to work on each pattern piece in isolation until some link was required with another piece. Although they required help with the computer operations, and had basic pattern cutting tuition, the production of the pattern was their responsibility. The intelligent way they solved their own problems on the pattern techniques by creating toiles at different stages was impressive, it was clear that this 'reality' was essential to their progress.

The qualities that they appeared to enjoy in computer pattern cutting were: accuracy of line and measurement, neatness, organisation, not having to struggle with paper, 'obvious if it is not right', 'the perfection of the printout sets a standard and makes you do it thoroughly', 'your mistakes are obvious', 'the brain knows what it wants to do but it can't do it as quickly as the computer'. It was interesting that at no time did they see the computer as controlling what they wanted to do, or placed themselves in a position where it dictated their creative actions. They appeared to limit the computer dictates to the organisation of data.

This may be related to the fact that they were all aware almost immediately of its insufficiency, this affected them to different degrees. To some it was a minor factor to others a prime concern, 'the work is distanced, it closes the imagination', 'human reaction and human skills are better for creative work'. All required the model stand at this early stage to get a 3D understanding.

The project of designing and developing an easy fitting shirt could be seen as a 'two-dimensional exercise' that posed few of the problems around the body form. Therefore, in the final practical session of the group's CAD experience, they were asked to draw an unusual sleeve design. They were then asked to go to the computer and make an approximate pattern for the shape. The shapes were plotted out and toiles produced, and it was apparent that the patterns had little relationship to the drawn designs. The students were asked to model shapes around a padded arm. There was little difficulty, the transposition to flat pattern shape could be seen. I believe that it takes many experiences of this nature before the brain builds itself the tacit knowledge of transforming from 3D concepts of 2D shapes. Two-dimensional CAD is not an effective substitute for working with the model stand and manual methods of pattern cutting.

One must recognise the context in which these students developed their skills and knowledge, and the advantages when compared with most college situations. They had personal access on demand to computers which *always worked*, they had computer and pattern technical support on demand, they also had access to manual tools and space within the same area.

Manual pattern cutting

The students rejoined the main group after their first term of the first year. It must be recognised that the students' reaction to manual pattern cutting, which took place in their second year, was affected by the different context in which they worked. Many of the comparisons they made were related to the lack of staff contact time programmed into the course, 'everyone seemed to be having a crisis at the same time'. It seemed that their organisational experiences on the computer assisted them. The word 'perseverance' seemed to be repeated frequently:

'we persevered more and seemed able to concentrate more.'

'manual pattern cutting it wasn't as bad as I thought . . . because I'd got the basic operations using a computer.'

'I persevered with it and I think we all persevered with it longer . . . more than people who had done it manually first of all . . . we knew the result you could get at the end . . . you knew that you could get it perfect and printed out at a quality, where if you have only done it by hand you leave it . . . but we knew the quality you could get from a computer pattern.'

'Although I came here with little experience I felt ahead of them anyway. Just basic things, like making a toile of parts to test out things.'

Another student who had no pattern cutting experience before coming on the course experienced some confusion:

'I was thrown in the deep end of it and wasn't sure what I was doing when I started . . . I couldn't relate it to what I had done previously . . . it was actually putting pen to paper and knowing what to draw . . . on a computer system you seemed to know what you were doing.'

It was noticed that the students who worked in a structured way on the computer, saw little difference between this and the way they approached manual pattern cutting, they stated that they would have liked more structure in their manual pattern cutting course.

Although the students were aware of the advantages of their initial computer experience, and all of them expressed a preference for working with the computer, they were unanimous that knowledge of the development of form had to come through manual pattern cutting experience, they believed that you could not develop this skill through the computer. This opinion was unanimous:

'or where do you get your intelligence . . . you have to learn by experience. When you have both you would go for the computer.'

'I see a 50/50 use of the computer . . . they are the same, you need the same intelligence but the stand and manual pattern cutting comes first . . . although manual pattern cutting is more time-consuming.'

The main group of students: Manual pattern cutting experiences

The students who were proficient in pattern cutting had no difficulty in the first or second year pattern cutting modules. The remainder found the experiences difficult:

'The second year was more difficult than the first . . . really frustrating. I deliberately did a very simple shirt in the first year . . . when I was given a photograph in the second year and asked to produce it, I felt I hadn't been trained to do that. The tutors could not get round everybody and as someone who had no pattern cutting knowledge it was very frustrating . . . you only had five minutes when they did get round . . . you wanted to learn, some people could get on with it. My only experience was first year needlework when I was eleven . . . it was very daunting.'

This graphic description, of large numbers of students and small staff contact, was repeated by all the students. However, one student found it easier in the second year 'because we were in pairs and didn't feel so helpless'.

The 'add on' CAD module: Both groups' experiences background information

The course offered two computer modules, one in each year of the course. The aims of Computers I in the first term of the first year were to introduce the students to the basic skills of computer use and to give an introduction to computers in the textile and clothing industries. The aim of Computers II was to extend appreciation of the use of computers in the textile and clothing industries, this took place in the final term of the second year and was set as an assessed project, there was also an examination. Both could be seen as 'add on' modules 'exported' out of the Department. The second module in Year 2 that included pattern development and grading was of particular interest.

The project work was originally discussed with the Course Leader in Clothing Studies, but the project was changed by the Computer Studies tutor without his knowledge. When the project was handed to students and they attempted to fulfil the demands, some elements were found to be irrelevant, unrelated to clothing manufacture and unmanageable. The project was hastily revised and, although still unsatisfactory in some areas, had to proceed. The module covered ten weeks and the Computer Studies tutor in charge gave the original seminars and lectures in the first four weeks, but as he had other commitments in research, mainly abroad, all the remaining taught sessions (three hours practical work per week for the fifty-three students on ten computers) were left in the charge of a third year Clothing Studies student on industrial placement in the computer room. The majority of the practical work had to take place in the students' own time in a computer room with no resident technical support available.

This description is deliberately factual, the situation amongst the students became very confrontational. The students' views of computers in pattern development are from interviews given at the end of the second year.

The students' views: The research group

The RGstudents' comments on their own performance:

'although there was a gap, the kick start at the beginning has enabled us to get on with things ourselves ... at an interview for a job last week, I went on a Lectra system and it didn't bother me at all . . . I am pretty confident.'

'it was over a year since I had done anything but it took me only half a day to cut my pattern and grade it.'

'I would have found it difficult to do if I had not had the early experience.'

'I managed okay, I had no problems.'

'I spent so much time helping other people, I had to rush mine in the end.'

They were concerned about the main group of students who apparently had great difficulty with the project. They thought that many of the main group now 'disliked computers because of their experiences'. All of them thought that the task was almost impossible for the main group to achieve because of the lack of facilities and technical support, 'How can they finish their job on time if the facilities are not managed'.

The students' views: The sample from the main group of students

The MGstudents comments on their performance:

'the research group have been so lucky in that it's so obvious that they are way ahead of us without a doubt. . . you could see the difference in the computer project, they were constantly pestered. It was a very frustrating unit very time consuming, those computers were in such a state because nobody was looking after them . . . people were losing work because they had viruses. The course has put me off computers, they are so daunting.'

'but there was just no-one . . . . lectures were very short . . . too much was assumed. Only two computers in the room actually worked with a rule library. Before we were given that project we should have been prepared. It should be more integrated into the course.'

'I was going off the whole idea after three days of problems with no help. I feel a bit more confident now.'

'if I hadn't had one of the research group as a partner I would have been crying and tearing out my hair . . . she taught me things I had no idea about. She deserves a medal, she taught so many things to so many people.

The panic you feel that you're going to fail because you have no help . . . you want to do your best but you can't do it because you haven't been taught . . . it's absolute panic. The course work should be part of the project. The project would have failed without the five.

I would love to be computer literate.'

'I really want to get into it but I got frustrated, I couldn't get the grading. We were left on our own, nobody there to identify the problems. Manipulation of the files is difficult. I did it by blind faith . . . didn't really understand . . . couldn't repeat it. The lecturer gave whole lectures on theories on bytes on the blackboard and then spent no time with you on the practical . . . just told to do it and no-one to help.

If I felt happier I would go on them, but I'm worried after the last experience.'

'I thought I understood the lectures and what we were supposed to do, but when we went in to do it, it went wrong . . . there was no-one there. Couldn't get support because the lecturer wasn't there. I enjoyed the pattern cutting/grading, I found it understandable, but I didn't enjoy the way the computers were always going wrong . . . it took all the enjoyment away. An hour's lecture then go away and do it, doesn't work. It must be integrated into the subject.'

The tutors' views: An evaluation of the teaching of CAD

It must be noted that the Course Leader inherited the curriculum form when he took over the course two years ago. He has revised the structure for the new intake and the computer elements are now integrated into the clothing units which make use of the technology and they are seen as part of an assignment. It must also be stated that the project brief for Computers II which he had accepted, was changed without his knowledge.

Three tutors were interviewed to understand their view of the Computer Module, Computers II; the Course Leader, the Design and Pattern Cutting tutor and the Computer Studies tutor. The interview covered three areas: the aims of the course, an evaluation of their success and the revisions that could be made.

The two Clothing Studies tutors saw the principal aim of the computer module as helping students to understand the inter-relations of CAD to all areas of clothing technology, and its close relationship with pattern methodology in mass production. The second aim was for students to acquire confidence in computer systems by gaining some familiarity with them. The Computer Studies tutor listed one aim, 'to gain familiarity and experience on a wide range of computer tools'. The list of the programs and what they offered was then given. When asked about how it related to the other modules on the course he stated that it was 'quite loosely'.

The Clothing Studies tutors were concerned about the students' understanding of the work that they were undertaking. Although they stated the same problem as the Computer Studies tutor of too many students, too few machines, and too little time allocated for a complex subject, the Clothing Studies tutors were more concerned with the module content. They believed that too much was expected in the hours allocated and that the work to be undertaken had little relationship to, or extended, the work in the main sector of the course.

> 'I think that they [the students] saw it more as an exercise rather than an industrial unit . . . we do try to make connections between one module and another . . . I wouldn't be at all surprised if students don't see any relationship between the two at all . . . essentially a sitting down process pressing keys.'

> 'they had a misunderstanding of the concepts of grading totally because of the project brief . . . they had done grading through mass production so they had never touched on anything to do with the individual.'

The Computer Studies tutor felt that the word processing section and the graphic section was well done but in the:

> 'construction and grading of the pattern I don't think they understood the mechanics of what was going on. Too little instruction on limited resources . . . too many students on too few computers and one practical session of three hours on a Tuesday afternoon . . . the best you can do is an hour each in pairs.'

> 'I think we are poor at assessing the amount of intellectual ability that they need to assimilate pattern grades and pieces. There is a whole range of intellectual tools that all of a sudden seem natural.

They need time and practice. You have to do something two or three times before it is assimilated.'

Revisions to the curriculum

The Clothing Studies tutors are already practising the following revisions with the new intake of students. Computers I to introduce students to the basic functions of computers remains. The Computers II has been dropped from the course and computers are integrated into the other Clothing units. The Clothing tutors state:

> 'computers really ought to be integrated into the units which make use of the technology ... the pattern development should be marked by assignment opportunities without it being seen as a separate block.'

> 'the team has got to sit down and address how it is to be taught ... what is a manageable number in a set? You don't have to give them that much extra. It is said that they have the feeling of inadequacy because of the management of the course.'

The Computer Studies tutor took a different view, 'I don't think you can put this into random parts of the course'. He saw the remedy in more time and practice, mastery of the computer, availability of equipment and smaller groups. With the present facilities, 'I don't think we can provide a high level technology input into the course'.

All the students encountered similar technical and equipment problems during the 'add on' module. The research group had enough basic knowledge in pattern cutting and the technology to overcome the difficulties. This fact was apparent to the main group. Comments from both groups of students for improvement of the course were basic and constructive:

(1) that the project is relevant to their other course work;
(2) that all students have to have a marked project on basics, 'people won't do it unless they have to do it', before they are given a complicated project;
(3) that the university should provide sufficient facilities to allow a project to be completed;
(4) that during projects technical support in the subject and computers must be to hand;
(5) that computer training must be done in small groups with one computer each.

An assessment of the difficulties of teaching CAD in pattern development

Most Fashion and Clothing departments, preparing students for careers in industry, recognise that CAD is an essential area of the subject that they teach. If the aims of the guidelines laid out in the introduction to this section are to be implemented fully it will not be an easy task. Creating this level opportunity is not easy, they are probably impossible without support from the highest level. The research projects have shown that even if a commitment is made, the hurdles are great.

The training and continual retraining of staff cannot be under-estimated; a beautifully functioning department can be wrecked by key staff changes and the integration of CAD into the curriculum adds to the complexity of timetables. Anything related to computers may therefore be delegated to the computer department of a college. The study showed that this can be contentious and worrying if the subject matter is specialised.

Providing enough equipment is a major problem, this will continually become out of date and require renewing. There will be high demands on the supporting technical staff just to keep the machinery running and updated. There is also a conflict between open access and the opportunity for theft.

It may be possible for large numbers of students to be introduced to basic or mechanical operations of CAD (i.e. grading and lay planning), by means of good manuals, videos, onscreen training programmes, good pre-preparation through computer-interactive lectures and manual techniques. However, if students are to develop towards self-sufficiency through individual project work, this requires a high staff ratio, particularly in the early stages.

Producing self-learning programs can be seen as an attractive option, but to undertake them to a professional level and avoid rote-learning packages, can consume hours of preparation time and requires an almost obsessional dedication from the tutors. The continual update of software programs can render these packages redundant within weeks.

Conflicting value judgements within departments can confuse students. However, they can recognise a prevailing view and a department's understanding of 'worth'. Marks towards the degree, is a priority amongst even the most idealistic students. CAD taught as a separate, unmarked or voluntary option or a lack of interest by staff in developing ideas using CAD, signals to students that it could be an alien and costly path to follow.

Endpiece: A personal view

Stake asserts that every aspect of an educational programme holds as many truths as there are viewers: 'Each sees value in a different light. The evaluator has no cause to force consensus, but certainly show the distribution of perceptions'.[6] It is impossible to strip research of personal bias, objectivity is rarely available in observational research. This endpiece is therefore stated as a personal view.

The principal motive for undertaking the study was an interest in the possibilities of teaching students the practical skills and knowledge of design and pattern cutting concurrently with knowledge of CAD. It became very clear that certain aspects of the knowledge, particularly procedural and organisational aspects can make a valuable contribution if it is integrated into any pattern design course. My present position, on developing the more complex perceptive skill of 3D transposition, is that it has to be achieved manually. Experiments with 3D pattern cutting on screen are immensely primitive at this stage and, I believe, only of academic interest in a discussion of immediate learning experiences on the type of technology readily available to tutors.

The second motive was an interest in examining any differences that might occur if students were taught in this manner. All the RGstudents developed an 'unexpected interest' in the technology and wished to use it in their future careers, two students managed to get industrial placements where they could use CAD. In the practice of the technology, it would seem from the views of all the students interviewed during the study, that perseverance, self-confidence and a practical competence in solving problems were the greatest gains for the research group. Their support and assistance to the main group during the practical section of Computers II was acknowledged by the MGstudents. Their positions in terms of marks gained in the practical work were not significant, approximately 10% above average and in their computer technology exam only marginally above average. The Computer Studies tutor stated that 'I don't think they have capitalised on their advantage, only one has shone through. I am disappointed in them, I was expecting to use them as catalysts in the class.'

Finally, it seemed important that there should be an examination of the effect of 'add on' computer modules. In over-stressed Fashion and Clothing departments it may appear tempting to 'export' the computer elements of the course. It would seem that if a department takes this course of action they should monitor 'not what the students appear to be doing, but what they are actually learning'. The aims and views of tutors from different disciplines in this study appeared to have very different priorities.

The organisation of the curriculum is being driven towards modularity. This appears to be taking place for 'management efficiency' with little debate taking place about its 'educational efficiency', and its effects in particular disciplines. The biological process that allows us to acquire knowledge is seen by leading researchers in this field,[7] as an intensely personal and holistic procedure in a constant state of change. Modularity may increase the breadth of access to knowledge, but a key element in the process of design is, I believe, about making connections. As knowledge in art and design is increasingly delivered in a set package form, who will be monitoring its effects in design education?

References

1. *Report of the Information Technology Working Party to the Committee of Art and Design*, CNAA Publication 2e/24, May 1983, p. 4.
2. The paper *Information Technology: Art and Design Policy Guidelines (1985) Concerning Course Design and Operation*, GENERAL/IT HAJ/ LM/HR, July 1985, issued revised recommendations from the 1983 working party, p. 0.
3. *Board for Design: Recommendations on the Incorporation of Information Technology into the Content and Teaching Methods of Design Courses*, November 1984, p. 1.
4. Aldrich, W.M. (1990) *New Technology and Clothing Design*, Ph.D thesis, Nottingham Trent University.
5. Ibid. p. 203.
6. Stake, Robert. (1977) 'The seven principal cardinals of educational evaluation. In *Beyond the Numbers Game* (Ed. by David Hamilton), Macmillan, London, 4.3, p. 188.
7. Edelman, G.M. (1989) *The Remembered Present: A Biological Theory of Consciousness*, Basic Books, New York; (1992) *Bright Air, Brilliant Fire*, The Penguin Press, London.
   Rose, Stephen. (1992) *The Making of Memory*, Bantam Press, London.

VIEWS ACROSS
THE CAD FIELDS

Chapter 12
CAD for
Clothing and Textiles

GAVIN WADDELL

Gavin Waddell is a designer and an educator. He studied fashion design at St Martins School of Art in London. He was an assistant designer to two of London's 'Top Ten' couturiers. He was the designer and director of his own couture house, ready-to-wear dress company and fashion forecasting concern. He was a menswear designer to a Kings Road boutique in the 1960s and a freelance illustrator and designer for many British and international companies.

Gavin Waddell was Head of fashion and textile courses at Luton, North East London Polytechnic and Gloucestershire College of Art and Design. He is a member of the Fashion Board for the Council for National Academic Awards and Business Technician Council. He is a member of the Society of Chartered Designers and he is an examiner and assessor to many fashion courses throughout Britain.

He became interested in CAD while designing a new course for Gloscat. This interest led to a piece of published research for the Science Research Council. He is currently a visiting lecturer on design at the University of Central England in Birmingham.

Introduction

My interest in CAD came about inadvertently, as a negative reaction to claims and assumptions I heard being made about my own subject – fashion design. Interested colleagues in other fields were applying their own attitudes and conclusions to my subject, and, I thought, clumsily applying these to a projected future of computer-led fashion design. I was so against these projections that I felt I must investigate the subject in a depth that satisfied my own professional conscience. I was, in fact, very sceptical at the outset, to the point where I questioned whether there was any future for CAD in the fashion industry at all.

I had been following the development of Computer Aided Manufacture and Computer Aided Technology (mistakenly so often referred to as Computer Aided Design) in the fashion industry for some time and had visited the very few companies that had installed computer aided lay planning, grading and in one or two cases computer aided cutting assemblies. The number of establishments that had any kind of computer technology could be counted on one hand.

Now under ten years later the number of computer aided units in the British fashion industry can be counted in thousands. I was particularly sceptical about the *quality* of design that could be achieved on the computer, having seen so many examples of the crude effects that had been perpetrated as 'design' in other fields, but was intrigued to find out what direct links were possible between CAD and the manufacturing process. As with much else I encountered at first, there was much talk but little hard knowledge except from those who were operating the systems 'on the ground'. Production managers and lay planners had taken over the role of directing the computer systems in the first factories I visited and they had become *very* knowledgeable indeed – knowledge acquired by trial and error, translating well-tried systems into a new language.

With a new race of technicians arising from this new technology, other roles in the fashion industry needed to be questioned and for my investigation the role of the fashion designer became crucial. Not only is the role of the designer put into dispute but the term design has very blurred edges, designers believing one thing, technicians another, the industry as a whole yet another and all further compounded by a general layman's view which has a rather romantic view of the whole activity. This would not matter to the designer were it not that any of these notions could affect the attitude and preconceptions of computer programmers planning new CAD systems for designers.

A research project in fashion design and CAD

This investigation later took the form of a piece of research for ACME – the Application of Computers to Manufacturing Engineering, a directorate of SERC, the Science Research Council – and was entitled

Strategic Study to Investigate the Opportunities and Difficulties in Fashion Design for Automated Manufacture. My collaborators on this project were Paivi Makerini-Crofts and William Bates.

Initially we interviewed a sample of fashion designers, representing as we thought the many different facets of the industry from the design directors of multinational companies and young designer-name companies, to design consultants and freelance designers. We looked again at the design process and what especially characterised fashion in this process. We reviewed the current fashion design CAD products. We wanted to know if there were aspects of computer automation which might de-skill a designer, and how the highly skilled designer could benefit from computer technology if there were plans afoot in softwear design houses for linking design into the existing computer aided pattern drafting, lay planning and grading systems. What design visualisation systems existed in other disciplines and could their techniques be applied to fashion? What future did the bureau design service have in design where small companies could buy time on expensive CAD/CAM systems. Could boring, repetitive time-consuming tasks be reduced, releasing the designer for creative design?

Designers on the whole were not sympathetic to the idea of computers, feeling that they could detract from, rather than enhance, the design process. They were worried about a loss of sensitivity and standardisation that the very character of a computer seemed to imply. Mechanical aids such as the stylus, VDU screen and plotter seem very far away from the soft lead pencil and the artist's drawing pad.

I concluded from interviews with designers and from the research generally, that the term design itself has its problems: the term has a completely different meaning to different people – designers, managers' technicians – in the fashion industry itself, let alone other areas of design. It is still under-rated and therefore defined in the lowest terms: 'stylist' or 'technician'. Its real innovative qualities are not understood even by practising designers, who quite often do not realise their real contribution to an industry that relies on their originality but is quite unprepared to acknowledge it. Technicians and production managers often see designers as a nuisance and the creative process as irrelevant.

I was also particularly struck by the fact that there appear to be two distinct *types* of designer, and not just in the fashion world. There is the designer who visualises the finished design in his head, is able to look at it from every angle, can make it walk up and down the catwalk, and sees the fabric, colour, cut details, buttons, trims, everything about it, accurately visualised and in a flash of a second. Then there is the designer who uses the sketch-book as a launch pad for new ideas; with this type of designer ideas come through drawing – very much in the manner of doodling – but carried to a much more sophisticated degree. This designer works from front and back views and therefore works in two dimensions. His translation to three dimensions takes place at the pattern cutting, toile making stage.

The former type of designer who visualises three-dimensionally, in advance, uses drawing simply as a method of realising an already conceived idea. The latter type uses drawing to invent, visualise and develop ideas still unconceived. These two types operate at quite different speeds and require quite different help from any mechanical or automatic aids, so the most appropriate CAD specification for one would not necessarily suit the other.

On the whole the development of current sketching programs for the first type of designer is quite inappropriate. These draw what he would term a 'pretty picture' – in other words a weaker presentation of something he already sees much more clearly in his head. He needs a three-dimensional modelling system to develop his already visualised idea. On the other hand the drawing designer could use adapted sketching systems to fit his design needs, but his drawing skills, sensitivity of line and personal techniques all help to invent his ideas and so far CAD sketching systems use conventional digitising tablets and stylus arrangements. Despite the latest innovations in more pressure sensitive pens, these systems lack the feeling of the 2B/HB/H pencil, rapidograph, brush, felt tip pen or even charcoal to help generate ideas on the pad.

It seemed to me that the second type of designer – the sketcher – was being catered for fairly adequately with the many sketching and paintbox systems on the market, but for the first type – the visualiser – and potentially the more interesting in terms of CAD development, very little had been done.

The nature of design and the CAD process

Because the real nature of design *is* either misunderstood or underrated and because it was so difficult to get beyond the barrier of salesmen to the true designers of the CAD systems, I found it difficult to get a true picture of the present state of innovation in the field. Many people talked about 3D systems but either did not really know about them or were loath to divulge information to an interviewer who could leak new and highly profitable ideas or methods to competitors. On the other hand the more expert the person I talked to, the more tentative they were about the present state of development in this design field. Most said that a form of 'solid modelling' was near the answer, but that the drape/hang/movement qualities still needed to be developed – and this development demanded so many variables in the writing of the software that the time and money involved have put many companies off. Michael Starling at SDRC, one of the leading experts on solid modelling in the industrial/product design field, said in 1988 that it would take two or three years' hard work on the part of an expert team of software writers and designers to come up with a system that would satisfy both the fashion designer and the manufacturer. He did however believe that an 'engineer-led' industry such as fashion needed to develop a comprehensive CAD system to match its CAM developments.

The missing links in the chain from the design conception to final production of garments occur at the beginning and end of this chain. CAD/CAM itself can be a misleading term as it does not explicitly describe the middle section of the chain which, in fact, has been the most developed in the fashion industry: pattern development, grading, lay planning, costing and cutting. Some very important work has been achieved in specific design fields; Clark's 3D shoe design system is a good example. As far as manufacturing is concerned it is only the cutting, spreading and conveying systems which have been fully developed and are in current and common use, although there is a lot of work going on in the field of robotic garment production. Juki of Japan is one of the leaders, and fully automatic robotic garment manufacture must become a reality sometime soon. However it was the design end of the chain that concerned our research, and it seemed that nothing really had been done in fashion that could compare with the work that has been carried out in engineering/industrial/product design where design systems can develop an idea in three dimensions from given specifications, can rotate, cover in a coloured skin, view from any angle in perspective and act as the model shop in the most sophisticated manner.

Graphics too have been similarly developed and are in everyday use, so familiar on our television screens. Architects and car designers were apparently using similarly sophisticated software. The difficulty with fashion is that it does not work in a rigid material like metal, plastic or concrete. Tweed, chiffon, taffeta, silk-jersey, acrylic and knit all move very differently and their hang and drape qualities entirely change the nature of a design. So far no real development has taken place in this area, presumably because the complex mathematical problems have yet to be overcome.

Types of design systems

Since the completion and publication of this research I have had the opportunity to look at an even more diverse range of computer aided design products, both here and abroad, and have tried to assess them in the light of our previous findings. There are three types of design systems currently available from software houses: the 2D design illustration/styling systems; the 2D illustration/styling systems that simulate 3D functions; and the actual 3D design systems. Most of the larger companies have integrated the first two, but only two houses – Computer Design Inc. in America and Modil in Belgium – have developed the latter, a truly 3D design system equivalent to the solid modelling packages available to product and engineering designers or Clark's 3D shoe design system.

Image creation

The 2D illustration system is most useful to the stylist designer who wants to sketch, visualise and produce attractive, saleable hard copy of his/her ideas in full colour with applied pattern and texture, much like a good colour photocopy. Most of the current systems have reached a level of sophistication that includes a huge colour palette, a fabric pattern and texture library, scanning and grabbing techniques and the possibility of scaling designs, patterns and textures up or down to a degree of accuracy that would never have been possible through manual draughtsmanship. For the commercial designer who needs to adapt and visualise, the possibilities are very encouraging. An image/figure design or diagram can be transferred to the screen either by drawing or tracing it on the digitising tablet or scanning it directly on to the screen from an existing drawing, illustration or magazine photograph. The 'brush' techniques are now so sensitive that the image can be drawn, coloured or adapted with a wide selection of 'brush' types that can simulate water colour, pastels, felt tip pen and broad or fine pen lines, can soften out hard edges and can erase unwanted areas. 'Brushes' can even pick up a texture either already in the menu or designed on screen; for example, a Prince of Wales or dog-tooth check in selected colourways could be washed over a design, or an all over multi-coloured print could be applied to selected areas.

Sequential designing

Sequential designing – that is where a basic design is tried out with, for instance, alternative collar shapes, cuff shapes or pocket placing – can also be practised on screen, although the pixel systems I have seen cannot yet make diagrammatic design quite accurate enough; the line always has an annoying wobble. The linear techniques used in most current pattern design systems are much more suitable for this kind of design and Ormus Fashion have developed a clever technique to overcome this problem. I understand, however, that the higher the resolution of screen and/or printer the less the wobble shows up.

3D design

As I mentioned previously, truly 3D design systems have only to my knowledge been developed by two companies, in the USA and Belgium. These are the fashion equivalent of solid modelling packages used by product and engineering designers, and can generate three-dimensional images from two-dimensional data. The wire framework so familiar in computer graphics is superseded at the American company by a 'framework' of dots which forms the basis of a sophisticated solid modelling technique. The 'framework' can take the form of a transparent tailored jacket or tailor's dummy, and style lines, panels, revers etc. can be plotted. The image can then be rotated and viewed from every angle. Using waist, hem and bust perimeters, a series of intermediate points can be generated including folds, bumps and curves. This 3D image can then be flattened into 2D diagram-pattern pieces.

The system I saw also included a skin function: the form can be covered in solid colour, print or weave – again all the visual effects we are used to seeing in computer graphics or solid modelling techniques, only with a fashion bias.

The problems regarding the hang and drape function (the algorithms needed to program these functions are, I understand, some of the most difficult to calculate) are not as it happens particular to fashion as the American company have worked with Chrysler on this problem to show the stretch and drape of car seat fabric, and are currently incorporating this function in their fashion design package. It appears that the hang could probably be given a specific gravity co-efficient which could, I presume, be matched with specific fabrics, say jersey, chiffon, taffeta, tweed etc. It should be added that I can find no British fashion company with sufficient confidence in 3D development to warrant their investing in a 3D system.

However, a 2D system can have all the essential function needed by the designer/pattern cutter; one such system, developed primarily as an educational tool for student designers by Ormus Fashion, allows the operator to match linear sketches on screen to a simultaneously drafted pattern alongside, developed either from adapted blocks already stored in the system or digitised from the designer's own blocks. A great advantage of this system is that it incorporates both linear and pixel modes. This means that diagrammatic design can be drawn in one mode and colour and pattern and texture can be applied in another obviating the disadvantages that these modes can have if used for the wrong purpose (as in the case of trying to draw diagrammatically with a pixelated line, which looks so very shaky). This system had some very interesting pointers for the commercial world and has subsequently been developed commercially for the industry.

The designers use of CAD

Fashion designers must overcome their reluctance and learn to practise with all these new tools provided by the computer. They must try out as many systems as possible before they or their company is persuaded to invest in one or other of the fashion CAD packages or even dismiss them out of hand and also have in mind the future compatibility that any CAD system will have with computer aided pattern design, grading, lay planning, cutting head, manufacture and conveyor functions.

With the great advances in CAD being made in printed and woven textiles, fashion designers will have to get used to, and be able to assess, the possibilities of fabrics generated and viewed on screen with only hard copy colour 'photocopies' as sample swatches.

Now that comparatively small manufacturing units in the fashion industry are finding it worthwhile to invest in computer aided grading, lay planning and cutting equipment as the price lowers and the flexibility increases, so design or what is inelegantly called the 'front end of the industry', must take up its rightful place in the CAD/CAM design-manufacture-distribution sequence.

The computer should mean the dawning of a new age for the designer, for the many constraints that have held the designer back in the past *could* now be overcome. Theoretically a designer could be housed anywhere, could design individual items, ranges or collections on screen, cut the pattern automatically, grade, lay plan and pre-set a complicated manufacturing program, all from the desk top. This would mean that many of the agonies of pattern cutter-designer liaison and production and manufacturing hang-ups were obviated, although this is not quite yet the case so far, but it could be.

However, fashion designers have not taken to computers. They feel they spell mechanicalness, conformity, a loss of artistic licence, a sell-out to the technological age which they do not feel they are part of and which has never been sympathetic to the designer's ethos. Much of this problem or misunderstanding is that, on the whole, hardware and software companies have not really taken the trouble to understand how the designer works or what motivates him/her. Software designers have *imagined how they think designers think and work*, have based assumptions on superficialities, like the appearance of the designer's sketch, and have built a whole complicated and expensive system around this false premise. They have looked only at the styling element of design – often just a recolouring, refabricating rerun of a 'lifted' design – and then fed this back to the designer as the ideal design package. No wonder the best designers have been put off; not only has their art been entirely misunderstood and misrepresented but no one even bothered to consult them. Presumably, from past experience in other disciplines, calculating computer companies have found that if they can sell their product to thrusting managing directors whose designers just have to fall in line, inevitable modifications and alterations required by the designers will be fed back to the companies automatically; although from my own enquiries, surprisingly companies seem to have been somewhat lazy in this department.

This was particularly brought home to me in our own research for the Science Research Council. There were of course some notable exceptions, as in the case where the system had been designed by a designer. I also understand that even in the case of the really sophisticated industrial design solid modelling packages, industrial designers are reluctant to use their systems. There is always the danger that a kind of uniformity appears to be achieved – a restricting format. The screen, its size and shape, the quality of line and colour, the inbuilt *style* of computer graphics – all these elements can be frightening to the designer and his fragile talent. None of these considerations, however, have been addressed properly by either the designers or the computer companies, and certainly not as they should be – by the two jointly.

In an age where even government is more concerned with presentation than content, it is probably little wonder that this 'King's new clothes' syndrome has manifested itself in some design thinking and has had a confusing effect on those who have to plan strategies for designers. The confusion between illustration drawing and design drawing (where the embryo design idea is brought to life) is further confused in computers by the sophistication of computer graphics: a discipline based on illusion – representing items that do not and need never exist. Drawing for design, on the other hand, is about items that will have to exist and the medium of drawing is used, by the designer, expressly to test, explore and specify an idea in reality and eventually of course into manufacture. This is further complicated by the phenomenon of the two types of designer that I outlined earlier. In many ways to test, explore and specify qualities of properties drawing are eminently suitable to the capabilities of the computer and are one of the areas that really need to be exploited in fashion design.

Companies are of course improving their systems all the time and it is interesting to look at particular companies and their specialities. A British company, Cybrid, for instance, has developed a pen/stylus that is cordless and can function for left- or right-handed operators. Its sensitivity and variable point pressure give it more the feel of pencil or pen. Hand to eye co-ordination is thus much improved because the natural hand movements of a designer (describing an arc with a single wrist movement, flow of line, variation of thick and thin line) are the nearest so far to the sketch pad and pencil. One of the great drawbacks of the digitising tablet and stylus has been its lack of 'feel' for the designer, who can overcome this by scanning in a previously drafted sketch rather than draw freehand on the tablet or trace over an existing drawing.

This same company has also developed a diagrammatic linear mode which means that curves, angles and straight lines can be drawn with a satisfying geometric degree of accuracy; and items such as revers, jacket hem curves and yoke shapes can be very much more convincing. In the pixelated mode any drawing of this type looks very clumsy. Colour mixing has become much more sophisticated and many different methods, or even choice of methods, are being offered by most companies. Many designers will have to brush up on their colour theory to exploit the systems to the full. Printout colour grid pages of real subtlety can be matched against paint, fabric or Pantone notation. Colours on screen can differ quite considerably from the chosen fabric sample, and although many companies are working to overcome this some operators can now do this adjustment in their head!

An American company who previously concentrated on CAD systems for knitwear now offer a full design system with a most interesting history of costume and history of art option (Moda Cad by Monarch Computex Corp). This means that a specific costume reference drawn from a large data bank, for example a 1959 Balenciaga dress, can be viewed on screen and used as direct design reference. Similarly the history of art package has references in the form of paintings, for example the Elizabeth I 'Ditchley' portrait by Marcus Gheeraerts, and in demonstration I was shown the embroidery from her skirt lifted to form the motif for a textile range.

The range of hard copy options is now quite impressive: an on-screen image can be photographed on a matrix camera, videoed on a print recorder, or using an extra high resolution thermal or ink-jet printer a printed image of very high quality can be achieved. The thermal and ink-jet printers have now largely superseded the others as they look most like a finished piece of designer's artwork.

Current use of CAD in the fashion industry

It is interesting to see how the fashion industry is actually using CAD. Margaret Newlands, the Product and Design Director at Jaeger, tells me that CAD has become an integral part of the design process for their company. They use it to recolour prints to house or season's colours, for the design of prints and printed scarves, embroidered T-shirt motifs, knitwear patterns, and even for shop merchandising to make sure a season's colour/fashion story is maintained throughout all the stores in the country. They have delegated all the CAD work to a most skilful CAD Systems Adviser, Josephine Hole, who inteprets the design team's needs on to the computer and can thus produce very high quality printouts of print ideas, border prints, embroidery motifs and knitwear designs to each designer's specifications. Their printer is of very high quality and resolution and the fact that it produces matt printouts almost indistinguishable from a print designer's gouache means that the design team do not have to adjust to a new set of visuals. They, like most companies that are experimenting with CAD, have only so far invested in a 'paint box' system, albeit of the most sophisticated type, and have it seems no plans as yet to try any of the 3D design/pattern making systems even though these in theory could feed directly into their computer aided manufacture. Further development is still needed to convince these large fashion companies.

Conclusion

Despite all these exciting possibilities, designers and the companies producing CAD packages, either through fear or meanness, have not yet collaborated to their mutual advantage. CAD producers seem to be afraid of the experienced vocal designer, preferring to employ and be advised by inexperienced college leavers who will not 'rock the boat' or ask awkward design questions, and who presumably demand much smaller salaries. Designers, on the other hand, are wary of a new and untried medium and cannot risk either their own or their company's investment in a very expensive product whose advantages have yet to be proved. This is short-sighted by both parties, for although the experienced designer would certainly want to ask awkward questions and change perceptions, he would, once won over, be the most convincing promoter.

Designers still reluctant to experiment are further put off by a sales pitch in which inexperienced demonstrators and extremely inept and inappropriate demonstration samples are the only means of judging the product's worth. Although student designers now have many opportunities to experiment on computers (most colleges have installed some type of CAD system) professional designers do not have this opportunity, and that time-worn phrase 'hands on' is still really the only method of understanding and judging the true potential that the computer can bring to design. More and more of our experienced designers should, somehow, be given the opportunity to experiment and discover for themselves the exciting potential of CAD.

Further developments

In the short time that has elapsed since I wrote the above – more and more designers and designer pattern cutters have become accustomed to computer aided design systems and now CAD, in some form or other, is a fairly everyday component of the fashion designer's repertoire – to the point where, in many cases, the designer and pattern cutter have, in fact, changed and adapted their skill quite significantly to the new technology. The majority of practitioners still, however, rely on their traditional skills and for them CAD companies have developed systems that will make this designer feel more at home. For instance an American company has designed a tabletop work surface that is just like the pattern cutter's regular drafting table where his/her usual skill and tools can be used in the traditional manner – for full size drafting, for freehand or instrument assisted drawing, measuring and correcting. The information, drafted on to the working surface in this manner, can be simultaneously fed into the computer system for grading, lay planning, storage or computer aided cutting.

Using an apparently quite different technology but with surprisingly the same result, a French company has just developed an electronic drawing 'sketch-pad' where the designer can sketch, draw, and colour as if on a drawing-board but with the added advantage that the information is being simultaneously assimilated by the computer system. Another advantage, where the more traditional designer is concerned, is that it obviates the difficulties of working on a digitising pad and observing the results on the screen which for many designers does not feel natural and disturbs their eye to hand co-ordination. It has to be added, however, that for those devotees of CAD now long converted to the digitising pad and VDU screen method, this 'sketch-pad' holds no fascination – they have adapted to such a degree as to prefer drawing on the tablet and observing on the screen.

These innovations do indicate a step in the right direction; it seems software designers are at last becoming more aware of how the fashion designer really works.

Acknowledgements

In order to gather the material to write this chapter I have had to survey, review or have demonstrated the following design systems:

Assyst-Assygraph, West Germany.
CDI Computer Design Inc., USA.
Cuttex, Switzerland.
Cybrid Fashion Designer, UK.
GGT. Gerber Garment Technology-Gerber Creative Designer and AccuMark Silhouette, USA.
Ivestronica-Inversketch, Spain.
Lectra Systems-Lectra Sketch 350+ and Graphic Instinct, France.
Microdynamics-MicroDesign, USA.
Modil, Belgium.
Monarch Computex Corp. Moda Cad, USA.
Ormus Fashion Education & Ormus Fashion Industrial, UK.

Chapter 13
Changing Attitudes: Towards the Virtual Future

KAREN MACHIN

Karen Machin has a B.Sc. in Civil Engineering and gained an M.Phil. in Computer Aided Drafting at Hollings Faculty, Manchester Metro University. She has experience across a wide range of applications on CAD systems for the clothing and textile industries. She has also developed computer programs, as well as using systems in industry. She is now working in CAD at the Royal College of Art, London.

Introduction

In the last edition of this book, I wrote of the need for a change in attitude towards computers from all the people working in the fashion and textile industries, not just the operators of the computers.[1] There was at that time a general atmosphere of technophobia as most people had limited access to computers and had no opportunity for first hand experience. I argued that this situation could not continue.

In the period since that edition was published there has indeed been a change in attitude of the population in general – even if we haven't got to a level where rioters loot the Powerbooks.[2] Manufacturers of CAD systems say that their new customers are more knowledgeable about the capabilities of the systems. Fashion and textiles students entering the RCA are significantly more computer literate than their predecessors of two years ago. The situation is improving quicker than I thought possible – the question now is how will it progress?

Current attitude towards the use of CAD

The use of computers in the fashion and textiles industry is led by the demands of production; computer aided manufacturing has been used for decades by those companies with the financial means to afford it. All the traditional benefits allow for the faster and more efficient manufacture of the finished product. Where the information from computer aided design (CAD) could readily be used to control this manufacturing process, there has been an enthusiastic response to the systems.

The textiles industry was quick to understand these benefits. With the small number of colours in the final fabric, be it a six-colour knit or a two-colour weave, basic computers with a limited range of colours could give an impression of the finished design of similar quality to the traditional instructions on graph paper. The speed with which samples could then be produced by computer controlled machinery gave CAD a major advantage over traditional methods. With more sophisticated computers and printers, capable of displaying millions of colours, it is now possible to control the shades of colour in each individual yarn to produce realistic simulations of woven or knitted fabric on paper and to print designs directly on to cloth, reducing the need for, and cost of, sampling still further. The benefits of up-to-date equipment provide an incentive for textile companies to invest in and upgrade their CAD system.

The fashion industry has not accepted CAD to the same extent as the textiles industries. With no direct link to the manufacturing of the final garment, CAD appears to be an expensive status symbol for the production of pixellated pictures by computer-literate youngsters. The traditional benefits of using a computer as an efficient tool, such as speed, accuracy and flexibility, are viewed with suspicion when the only direct output is an A4 paper printout.

This is not to say that CAD has no possible current function for the fashion industry – for some companies it can enhance their method of working. Where presentations, storyboards and illustrations are a major function of the design department, the speed and flexibility of the computer are an improvement over the traditional pen and paper, but many companies do not produce such a quantity of illustrative work. The designer, working closely with the pattern cutter, may translate the original idea from the sketch directly into cloth with no need for a detailed illustration. Most small designer companies would not justify the expense of computerisation in comparison to the traditional methods – at the moment.

Just as word processing has become the accepted norm, so drawing on a computer will be seen to be the most efficient method of working. This has already proved to be the case for specific industries such as graphics and textiles where the results of the CAD design are required for the later production processes. Must the fashion industry wait for a similar link to manufacturing before accepting CAD? For the day when the press of a button translates the design sketch into the required pattern pieces or garment?

The need for general computer awareness

The overall attitude towards computers does seem to be improving in that there is less technophobia. Now that manufacturing systems are proven and CAD systems are proving to have benefits for some techniques of working, there is increasing pressure to computerise, and a corresponding growth in the number of trade shows and exhibitions, articles and books, to provide information on these essential tools. But there are still buyers who, eager to own a computer because it is the latest trend and impressed with sales demonstrations of the ultimate gadget, discover later that these are not easily integrated into their existing methods of working.[3] It is unrealistic to be satisfied with the current state of computer awareness when this organisational problem can still be identified. Although computers may appear to be the latest trend there are still associated problems and, I believe, these could be reduced by a wider awareness of the computing field.

It has often been said that CAD systems for clothing are designed by computer programmers who have no knowledge of the specialist way of working. But who is to blame for this lack of dialogue? Both industries seek an immediate return from the conversation, with one aiming to find new markets for existing products and the other eager to try the latest offer of help. The computer companies often employ someone with the expertise to communicate between the two fields and sell their product. The opposite does not exist, the fashion community rarely has the foresight to employ anyone with computer-related knowledge other than the system operators. Research and development is left to the suppliers even though there are so many complaints about their supposed lack of awareness. Management, the people with the overview of their company operations, are from a generation which often boasts unashamedly of its illiteracy of computers. With a lack of interest in the wider issues of computing, it is impossible to suggest far-reaching changes to the systems and the long term company view will be inaccurate.

Technological fashion

How many in the fashion world are aware of the subjects of current discussion in the computer world? It is hard to have any hope when it is still impossible to find a fashionable outfit with the essential pocket for a personal stereo. And if it is impossible for fashion manufacturers to consider a fifteen-year-old piece of technology, what hope is there for the future?

Students, young people more familiar with computers, do they see any links between fashion and technology? Set them a project to design garments for the future, and they predictably dash out and read their William Gibson.[4] There is an immediate understanding that technology will be a major influence. Their work is not limited to ideas of techno-styling, they look to the ideas of science fiction writers for inspiration on a new functionality for clothing. They take on board the idea of technological fashion to produce sketches of futuristic garments with minimal current practicality. But I wonder, how do we get to the point where this sort of idea could be reality?

Fashion does of course coexist with the rest of the world and when there is a demand for a new type of clothing it can react accordingly and the garments are on the shop rails as soon as possible. Where this influence is from a traditional field, such as the trends from the latest international fashion shows, the clothes can be on the High Street within weeks. Although I doubt whether any of these international designers use CAD. One look at the trends showing yet more retrostyling or another season of deconstructed garments leads to the depressing conclusion that there is indeed nothing new originating from the fashion community. Anything vaguely modern seems to be an application of new yarns or techniques for dyeing and finishing, subjects closely linked to fashion. There seems to be no communication with the rest of the world, with the advances being made in other fields.

What would happen if technological advancement from a non-traditional field required fashion input? As the barriers between different disciplines are broken down, with specialists from each working together on a project, so fashion must become more involved with other fields. As an example, much of the work on wearable computers may belong to the electronics industry, but wouldn't input from the fashion community be of benefit? Unfortunately, with the lack of awareness of computing and its concepts and language, a dialogue would still be inconceivable. How long is it going to take for the fashion and textiles industries to catch up with ideas of multi-media, voice and gesture recognition, agents, networked communications, portability and virtual reality? Where are the fashion designers who could show direction in the application of today's technology and understand the implications of and provide the lead towards an aesthetics for tomorrow's technology?

Virtual fashion

One topic undergoing much discussion and research in the computer world is that of Virtual Reality (VR) and cyberspace.[5,6] Whether these are 'hip, hype or hope'[7] has been debated, but their development is most definitely taking place with games manufacturers already having immediate financial benefits from the systems. VR is not just another games machine for teenage boys to lock themselves further away from the reality of the everyday. There are existing commercial applications for visualisation in architecture and interior design. Could this technology be applied to fashion?

The popular image of VR is not one that would appeal directly to the fashion community. With a public image derived from articles detailing its potential as a dangerous enhancement for sex, war and recreational drugs and photographs of VR users wearing cumbersome helmets and gloves attached to computers by heavy cables, it is hardly likely to appeal to a fashion community attracted to the finer qualities of cut, drape and texture.

But VR will have an effect on the fashion and textiles industry. It will alter the methods used for clothing design and construction, it will be used as a presentation tool, as an aid to range building and marketing. Already, with the limited tools available, there is work on the virtual catwalk.[8,9] Retailing will also be changed with computerised catalogues showing the way towards remote shopping.[10] And what effect would the domestic use of VR entertainment systems have on the clothing market itself? Would you bother to invest in skiwear for that two week holiday if you could ski in the comfort of your own home when you felt like it?

Whenever I have expressed an interest in the subject, the usual reaction is an assumption that the fashion industry could be allowed a role in the design and manufacture of the data gloves and body suits required for VR interaction. These accessories are frequently referred to as 'computerised clothing'. The data glove or suit encompasses the wearer and provides information to the computer about the position and gestures of the participant. These datasuits are currently un-flattering, undesirable garments; certainly only the most dedicated cyberpunk would want to wear one every day. With further work on the electronics there is no reason why they cannot be reduced to portable accessories as normal as stereos or telephones. Or they could become more stylish, wearable and fashionable, normal parts of everyone's wardrobe; every person owning their own selection of styles, colours and fabrics as with any other garment.

It is true that the fashion industry could be involved in the pro-duction of these garments and could be looking at how garments can be used to interact with computers. However, the consequence of the development of VR will be more than the specification of these interaction accessories. Fashion is concerned with the appearance and image of the human person. The clothes we wear are important for communication to other people, many assumptions being made by first impressions, our dress code. Expertise from this field should be involved in the creation and design of the appearance of people in the virtual world.

Worlds containing representations of people have been developed for telepresence and entertainment. With telepresence, you become the robot at the other end of the computer control. Here, if you appear at all, you are as yourself photographed using a video camera. In games you take on the persona of a games character – a fighter plane or a character such as an elf. You cannot as yet change your appearance – there is no interaction which affects your graphical representation. Your appearance is selected by the computer pro-grammer who designs the virtual world and that person will have different values to yourself. This takes away your choice of how you represent yourself, something most people enjoy in the real world and a power they do not readily relinquish. However, since a body image is in itself a 3D object in the virtual world, there seems to be no reason why there could not be interaction to change appearance. If you can create your own world, it should be a simple matter to dress yourself.

The nature of appearance in the virtual world does not seem to have been considered as yet in the research field of Virtual Reality. The computer programmers, scientists, anthropologists and psychol-ogists involved do not appear to be overly interested in this question – they seem content to represent people using shorthand objects such as a sphere or a floating glove, and many people in the fashion community would comment on the real world nature of these scientists' appearance. Such questions as 'what can I wear?' do not seem a priority.

Unrealistic representations of the participant are partly due to the difficulties involved in modelling and animating the human figure and the drape of textiles. The number of mathematical calculations and size of computer memory limit the level of detail for the model especially in real-time applications. There is however sufficient interest from the leisure industry, from film and game producers, for the development of realistic models to take the place of human actors. But would you necessarily want to be represented by a realistic simulation of yourself? Why be limited in your ideas of appearance when you have left behind such everyday details as sizing and washing instructions? If you could use VR for entertainment, a remote social event such as a nightclub, wouldn't you perhaps want to be seen in the most creative disguise?

There is no doubt that the appearance of objects will take a greater significance as we become familiar with this new language, exchanging pictorial information on an electronic network. The level of involvement of the fashion industry should be more than the production of desirable datasuits. The fashion industry should be involved in all developments concerning the representation of human appearance, but this would only be possible with a wider understanding of computers, an understanding which is rarely seen at the moment.

Conclusion

With foresight from the knowledge of anticipated computer developments, aside from the mundane of faster and cheaper, companies can make confident predictions of the future for their own computer investment. With this wider knowledge they would see that their problems are not unique, that other industries have had similar difficulties to those that fashion and textiles are experiencing at the moment. They may also see methods of working that could be applied to their own business, applications of computers to which they hadn't been introduced, and an overall view of technological advances which could provide a new source of inspiration.

Computers are already altering not just the way we work, but also the way we think of ourselves. As we rely on these electronic tools for an increasing number of functions they start to become an extension of ourselves, their memory becoming an essential supplement to our own. And, just as they are already affecting our function, so they will also begin to alter our sense of how we look, our appearance. This is the concern of the fashion industry.

After all, if she works in Virtual Reality, what does she wear to work? And what does she look like at work? And whose is it?

Notes

1. Machin, K. (1992) Changing Attitudes. In *CAD in clothing and textiles*, Ed. by W. Aldrich. Blackwell Scientific Publications, Oxford.
2. W. Gibson describes watching the LA riots of 1993 on television and seeing the crowd leave the Applecentre untouched amongst the surrounding devastation, in V. Allen, 'Life after cyberpunk', i-D magazine, October 1993. Powerbook and Applecentre are trademarks of Apple computers.
3. Robson, D. More vision, less dazzle. *Design*, May 1993.
4. Gibson, W. *Neuromancer, Count Zero, Mona Lisa Overdrive, Burning Chrome*. Grafton, London.
5. Laurel, B. (Ed) (1990) *The art of human-computer interface design*. Addison Wesley, Wokingham.
6. Rheingold, H. (1991) *Virtual Reality*. Secker & Warburg, London.
7. The title of the discussion panel at SIGGRAPH 1990, described in B. Woolley (1992) *Virtual worlds*. Blackwell, Oxford.
8. Gray, S. (1992) CAD conference, London, Textile Institute, December 1992.
9. P. Old, MA project, Royal College of Art, described in N. Niesewand, Live wires . . . computers byte back. *Vogue* (UK), September 1993.
10. Sherman, B. (1992) *Glimpses of heaven, visions of hell*. Hodder & Stoughton, London.

Index